A  ADVENTURE

MOVE YOUR ASS!

YOUR EASY GUIDE TO CHANGING YOUR OUTLOOK TODAY

J.D. GEORGE

*For my wife, my children and all the special friends
that help me to live a positive life.*

CONTENTS

AS A SUCCESSFUL BUSINESSMAN FOR NEARLY MANY YEARS, I look back at one of the most important aspects of my life—having a positive attitude. I remember, years ago, reading books, articles, and listening to tapes all about positivity, the problem was they all had catchy slogans and short-term solutions. They were the equivalent of a five-hour energy drink. I needed something that taught me the skills to live a positive life for my entire life.

I realized early on that negativity was not going to get me where I wanted to go in life and that my goals in business, and in my personal life, could not be achieved by short-term "trendy" solutions. With all that in mind, I set out on a journey to build the foundation and skills to live a more positive life, for the rest of my life. I achieved many business and personal goals as I went, including my most significant goal of supporting my wonderful family, always my core motivating force. This outlook allowed me to accomplish many other goals including starting a business, running a marathon, and learning many new skills and hobbies.

Through the years, I continued to experience that living with positivity was working, people with similar views and I gravitated to each other, and we formed the Personal Positivity Network, dedicated to studying and teaching people how to use the power within themselves to accomplish all they wanted to in life. Many people have talked or written about how a positive lifestyle can be beneficial in numerous ways, we wanted to create a path to making positivity a lifelong journey. We decided that we would complete the goal of writing a book in which we would share the keys to building a foundation for living a very fulfilling life in which you could accomplish more (in your business and personal life) than you had ever anticipated.

In the upcoming guidebooks, we will teach you to change you outlook today! We believe the ability to do this gives you a "superpower" that we have fun calling Pozzam! You will embark on a journey with a number of steps that build on each other, but the first is to *Move Your Ass* and get started!

We strongly recommend, if you have not done so, you sign up for the accompanying automatic Daily Affirmation texts and the Bonus materials at *WWW.POZZAM.COM/DAILY.*

OWN IT!

WHO DOESN'T LIKE SUPERHEROES? Superman, Supergirl, Spider-Man, Wonder Woman … they all have at least three things in common. Obviously, there's the superpowers. And of course, the really great costumes. Finally, and perhaps most importantly, the superheroes we've all looked up to as kids and perhaps even now, share one unifying trait: positive energy—tons of it! No matter how many times they get knocked down, they get right back up again. When was the last time you saw Wonder Woman whining about not being back home, sulking, complaining, or pouting? It just doesn't happen. Superman doesn't let the idea that Kryptonite exists get in the way of his success or stop him from believing there IS a way to achieve what he needs to.

But here's the thing. That Positivity? It's not just for those of us walking around with a Lasso of Truth or the ability to shoot lasers out of our eyes. Sure, those Superpowers are pretty great—but what if you had your own? We believe you do. It's that same unifying trait that resides in all the heroes we look up to—it's the power of Personal Positivity.

Personal Positivity is an outlook, a new approach to life and to the situations we all face. It's the key that unlocks the door you've insisted is standing between you and that wonderful lifestyle you aim to lead.

Through Personal Positivity you can change how you deal with challenges and stressors; you can adjust your perspective on life itself. It helps you see opportunities more readily and have the courage to jump on them, it gives you the energy you need to explore more of what life has to offer. It equips you to overcome fears, take more risks, and go after your dreams, goals, and desires.

It can lead to a wonderful lifestyle. Through Personal Positivity you will have a new perspective on the world. You will be able to reach new personal heights by shedding baggage from the past that's holding you back. Instead you'll find yourself living in the now, planning for your future with enthusiasm as you reach your full potential. Personal Positivity will propel you forward to grow and expand your interests and activities. You will enjoy deeper and more satisfying relationships and feel a greater sense of fulfillment in your life. In short, you will be happier and more productive. The truth is, Personal Positivity challenges you and allows you to get the most out of every day.

Some of you may be thinking, there are a lot of wonderful messages out there about Positivity in books, lectures, articles, webinars, blogs, and so forth. Many people are discussing the impact of Positivity, so what makes this program any different?

The difference is that while these books, webinars, and so forth are quite uplifting, the message, which is well-meaning, doesn't last for very long. Sure, you will put down the book, or leave a webinar, feeling pumped up and full of Positive energy. But as you return to life's challenges, the enthusiasm begins to fade. The fact is, life will throw you a bunch of curveballs and since the book, seminar, or webinar has not provided you with a solid foundation to build upon, or helped you establish a skill set to effectively deal with such curveballs, you won't have the tools you need to deal with these challenges. It's like going on a retreat with your team at work to improve work culture. The two or three days of the retreat are full of positive messages and team building. Everyone leaves with smiles on their faces, ready to forge ahead as a team. However, after a few days, perhaps a week, the feeling wears off. Typical issues arise at work, and suddenly it's back to business as usual. This is because the Positive feeling is like a five-hour energy drink. You get a burst of energy and your heart starts racing. You feel great for a while, but in time you come crashing down and may even have less energy than when you started. This is because making changes, like most important things in life, takes time, preparation, and hard work. When you are truly committed to making Positive changes in your life, you prepare for the speed bumps as you ride along the road to success and happiness. For this to happen you have to keep working at it. Fortunately, the process detailed in the adventure you're about to embark on here will help you prepare and keep you working, holding you accountable for those changes and making sure that they actually happen. For real this time.

This adventure is uniquely designed to guide you through a step-by-step process that gives you a foundation for long-term change. Few people looking to enjoy a more positive and productive lifestyle have trained themselves with a process that provides lasting power to face life's challenges and seize opportunities. That is what this adventure presents: training to improve your life through Personal Positivity.

Truly successful and accomplished people put in the hard work it takes to succeed. Athletes, performers, entrepreneurs, medical professionals, among others, achieve success through dedication, repetition, and a positive attitude.

Some people are born with great natural talent and abilities. However, many of these very gifted people never fully reach their potential. They do not have the attitude or work ethic necessary to accomplish great things. Those who win forge forward, constantly honing and perfecting their skills and abilities. This process is no different. It may take weeks, months, or even a year, but in the end it will be worthwhile.

This book will take you on an adventure, and over the course of this adventure you will build the foundational habits for leading a life with the power of Personal Positivity. We all have the natural ability to access this power, and through this adventure you will find the steps to fulfill your potential.

YOU ARE IN CONTROL

What made you reach for this program? Something led you here, something pushed you to sign up, but what was the real motivation? Perhaps you have let too much negativity into your life. It's possible you are letting negative people influence you and get you down. Perhaps you are dissatisfied with your personal relationships, or you're unhappy with your physical health. You may be disgruntled with your job and your income. Maybe you are getting bored with your current interests, activities, or the people with whom you hang out. You might be blaming your life situation on your lack of education, your parents, your culture, your lot in life, your relationships, your boss, lack of money, the economy, politics, the country, or the world.

When one, or several, of the factors above causes us to think negatively, we often just give up and say, "There's nothing I can do about it." The truth is, there is something you can do about it, but it starts with changing your attitude.

The good news is that you are interested in making a change; you want to become more positive and effectively manage life's pitfalls. The question is, are you ready to commit to this process? Making a personal commitment starts by recognizing that this is a journey, and like most journeys, it starts with small steps. It also means recognizing that you, and only you, control what you think. No one else is responsible for your thoughts but you. Sometimes, with the pressure of bosses, spouses, family, friends, and the media we forget that we each have control over our own life. Take a moment to think about it, really think about it: no one, not a single person, can make you think something unless you allow them to. If someone is making you feel inferior, making you doubt yourself, or making you think you are not the beautiful person you are, that is because you are allowing them to do so.

You are in control of your thoughts and actions, nobody else. Don't give someone else the power to be in control. People cannot control other people's minds. The fact is, the only thing we truly have 100 percent control over is our minds, our thoughts, and our attitudes. The only one who can control you is you!

In addition, only one person is responsible for your life situation, your job, your health, and your relationships, and that's *you*. It's important that you understand you have the power and can change anything and everything in your life: your thoughts, your situation, your success, your happiness, your friends, your relationships, and your future. Then, and only then, will you be ready to make the changes to accomplish anything you desire. It all comes from inside of you and nobody else. That's when you can say, "I got this. I own it."

Now, stop reading for a moment and say to yourself, or even out loud, "*I own it!*"

By doing this, you are taking control and fully embracing the concept. At this point you are truly in control of your life and ready to start out on the Pozzam Adventure.

FROM DEAD-END JOB TO DREAM CAREER: TAKING OWNERSHIP

Consider the story of Denise. One day Denise, a 30-something mother of two living in Pennsylvania, was waiting as a friend did some repairs on her car. He started talking about a home nearby and how he wished he could own it someday. Denise, who was working in a dead-end job that she did not enjoy in the slightest, sat and listened, thinking that maybe one day she too could own such a home. Even better, maybe she could sell homes for a living. Denise had grown up in a poor, run-down neighborhood, but she always had a fairly positive attitude about life. She wanted to believe good things could still happen for her if she was open to making changes. Denise said to herself: if something is going to change, I have to change it, I have to own it.

Later that afternoon, once her car was repaired, Denise made a very small change in her life. She bought a book on how to sell real estate to read every night. It was a very simple change, but one she thought could push her forward. So, each night after her boys went to sleep, even though she was exhausted, she sat up and read at least ten pages rather then watch television. When she finished the book, she made another change—she decided to take a class on how to get a real estate license. She did that, too. Denise soon realized the power to make positive change was in her own hands. So, with that mind-set she made another change—she decided to study rigorously for the real estate exam. She worked hard and had a positive attitude. Rather than dwelling on her dead-end job and letting it bring her down, she took ownership of her life and found a new goal, to become a real estate agent. When one of her boys asked her if she was going to pass her real estate exam, she said, "Don't worry. I got this."

Fast-forward a few years. After passing the exam, Denise used the sheer power of Personal Positivity to sell more than 70 homes in two years and win several awards in sales. From that first conversation with the mechanic, she had two choices. She could have decided that becoming a real estate agent was too difficult and do nothing about it, or she could set a goal for herself, take ownership, and follow the path to discovering a new life. She came to believe that she and only she controlled the making of these positive changes.

When she started selling homes, both home buyers and sellers loved working with her. Where they saw problems, she saw solutions; when they got caught up in negative thinking (this house will never sell), she told them why it would sell—and she turned out to be right. The result for Denise was not just monetary success, but today Denise is happier than ever before, knowing that she did it all by herself. Denise took ownership of where she was, made no excuses, and went about changing things. She started with the first small change, reading ten pages of the real estate book each night; only she could do that for herself. It all started with her deciding: "I am in control. I own it." She possessed the Superpower of Personal Positivity.

TAKING THE FIRST STEPS TO POSITIVE CHANGE

You have to put in the work to get the most out of this process. As the saying goes, anything worth achieving takes time. Making real life changes takes time. It also takes incremental steps, small changes, to make big changes. In time, you are going to make some very big changes, but you must start off with smaller ones.

What better example, when it comes to taking baby steps, than to think about the process babies use when they learn to walk? They don't just stand up one day and decide they're tired of crawling, so from now on they're going to walk. Instead, they take a few steps; they hold your hand or hold on to the couch as they make their way along each day until they get the hang of walking. They will fall down once in a while, but they are making a positive change, from crawling to walking, and it takes time. Such small steps are necessary for making improvements throughout your whole life.

Two initial parts are involved in making positive changes. For part one, we need to take control and decide on something we would like to do that involves making a small positive change. Then there is part two, actually doing it. You need to start off with a very small change that is important to you; this will be one of the exercises at the end of the Guidebook, so start thinking about it. From eating healthier to getting more fresh air, from engaging in an activity you simply enjoy to learning about an area of interest, you can take a small step today, and start making a small change.

For example, you might decide it's time to take better care of your teeth, so you decide to start flossing every day. That's it, nothing more. Just take four minutes and floss every day. Perhaps you'll decide to eat something healthy each day, like a piece of fruit. Maybe you will decide to have four glasses of water each day or take a daily walk. Perhaps you want to work on something that simply makes you feel better, such as making your bed, or playing a musical instrument. What is something simple, and positive, you would like to change? What simple change could you make starting today?

MAKING CHANGES 101

After you decide what to change, you need to do it and then continue doing it. This is easier said than done. Many of us will do something new on Monday, and maybe again on Tuesday, but by Wednesday we forget. By Thursday we are so preoccupied with something else that it takes us away from making even the smallest of changes. So, what can you do to make a change last? Write it down and post it someplace where you will see it every day—like on your refrigerator or the mirror over the sink in your bathroom. You could use the Reminder app on your smartphone. After five or six days it will get easier to remember with or without the reminders.

Researchers say that it takes about three weeks—21 days—to form a habit. These are positive habits, so whatever you choose, go for it, do it! If you skip a day, just get back to it the next day. Be careful not to let skipping days become the habit.

By starting with a small change, you will realize that change isn't so difficult after all. A small change is a great example of the control you have over yourself, control you might never have realized you had. Remember, the ability to make a positive change is inside all of us. We just need to start utilizing it. As you proceed and follow this process you will see great comfort through small changes and gain the confidence that you can make changes. But I warn against setting goals that are too big or major changes just yet. You will get there, but you are not ready. Setting goals or making changes that are too big at first can be riddled with frustration. Plus, there may be setbacks, but don't worry, you will learn to deal with such setbacks in upcoming Guidebooks. For example, running a marathon is not a small step by any means; it's a very big step that starts with many, many smaller steps, such as getting in shape, building up your stamina, running one mile each day, then two, then five, and so on. Losing 20 pounds is also not a small step; it requires a lot of work overtime, as is the case with starting a business, which can be very complicated. All of these major changes are within your reach, but you have to build up to them.

Your small change should be something simple that you can do every day, even without seeing any immediate results. The "win" will be in doing something new, in making that initial small change, which will make you feel great. The results will come. Now don't worry, you did not invest in this program to just learn to floss every day; bigger things are coming, but for now we just want you to experience the positive effect of change.

FIND THE POSITIVES AND BANGING AWAY AT THE NEGATIVES

One of the fundamentals of Personal Positivity is recognizing that you have two options when it comes to your thoughts: your thoughts can be positive or negative. Therefore, a critical first step toward Personal Positivity is learning to recognize negative thoughts. You want to recognize and acknowledge such negative thoughts when they appear. These are thoughts that drag you down, distract, discourage, infuriate, frustrate, or even make you feel a sense of hopelessness and despair. These negative thoughts get in the way of forward progress. Often you are dwelling on things that happened in the past that you cannot do anything about.

After you recognize negative thinking, you need to learn how to handle the negative thoughts. One method is replacing such thoughts with positive ones. This is not always easy, but you need to be persistent and sometimes you must "bang away" at negative thoughts.

For example, you may be going about your day and suddenly start thinking negatively about your boss, or someone else you know. Perhaps you start remembering a bad experience that happened in the past. You need to push this out of your head by replacing it with more positive, forward-thinking thoughts. Remember, it's not easy; so be diligent and keep banging away, by trying to push the negative thoughts out with positive ones. When you want to shout at your boss, instead think about the great times you enjoy with your colleagues going out after work. The same thoughts may come back later in the day, so again you need to fight negativity over and over again. At first it will feel like a battle raging on in your head, but don't get discouraged; keep up the fight.

To push out negative thoughts effectively, you want to have some positive thoughts at the ready. Stay focused and aware of your positive thoughts. This will be hard in the beginning, but as you learn to approach every situation with your power of Personal Positivity, it will get easier.

Remember, there is always a positive approach. For instance, you might have been planning your day around going out on a boat trip, but when the day arrives, it's pouring rain and it makes boating prohibitive. The negative thoughts are the day is ruined, your plans are ruined, now you're going to have to stay home and it will be a boring day. Instead of moping and thinking about how bad the day will be, you can push out the negative thoughts with positive ones, such as now you can curl up on the couch and finish the book you've been reading, perhaps you can talk with (or text with) an old friend, or this could be a perfect day to binge watch a Netflix show.

It's all about your mind-set. You can think negatively and feel bad that it is raining, or you can take a positive approach. You must train your mind to focus on positives instead of thinking about negatives. Instead of sulking because you didn't pass an audition, or land a client at work, bang away at the negatives. Think about finding more auditions or ways to start looking for new clients. As Alexander Graham Bell is credited as saying, "When one door closes, another one opens." That's positive thinking. There's always a positive if you look for it.

If you are having trouble finding positive things to focus on, then stop and think about what and who makes you happy. What's your favorite food? Where do you feel relaxed and happy? Who makes you laugh? What makes you feel good? Some people love their work, others love their hobbies, and many people love thinking about their friends and families. Focus on the people, places, and things you like to do. You can even use outside influences to put you on the positive track. It can be something very simple. Perhaps you saw a funny movie the other night. If you are mired in negative thoughts, focus on the movie that made you laugh.

Note that positive thoughts are not "I hope so-and-so gets fired," or "I'll get even with him/her." Revenge, or retribution, is *not* a positive thought or action.

It all comes down to your attitude and how you approach a situation. As you go through this process, you will reach a point where you can flip the switch from negative to positive thinking. We all have a switch within us that lets us make the decision to change our way of thinking. In time, the switch will become automatic and you immediately start focusing on the positives. Always remember you control and own your own thoughts. The process of replacing negative thoughts with positive is the start of taking that control and owning your thoughts.

Still there will be times in life when you will feel sad or angry. It's perfectly natural to feel bad if you have lost your job, have a sick friend or family member, or have another legitimate reason to be upset. Bad things happen. The idea is not to ignore your emotions or pretend negative aspects of life do not exist. It's okay to feel sad when you hear bad news or when something upsetting occurs. After all, you are human.

The important question is: after feeling sad for a while, can you then find a positive way to move forward? Can you move away from the negative thoughts? The practice of Personal Positivity allows you to go through a period of sadness and return to positive thinking. Make no mistake, the feelings are your own, you own them, too, and you have every right to embrace your feelings. Later in the adventure we will discuss how to deal with your feelings and emotions and how to harness their power with the power of Personal Positivity.

As you proceed along the path to Personal Positivity, by putting in the work, you will find that it gets easier to think of positive thoughts. Remember, you will reach a point where it is second nature to think positively. This is when you truly begin to control the Superpower that is Personal Positivity.

We've talked about taking small steps on the path to Positivity and that there is a lot ahead of you. There are also some small actions that can help you along the way, and one of the simplest is so simple ... you can smile.

SMILE

Starting to make a change can begin with a simple smile. It sounds silly but it's true.

While smiling may not solve anything, it's hard to be too negative with a big smile on your face. Smiling several times during your day will simply make you feel a little better. You'll also find that if you smile at other people, most of them will smile back, which makes both of you feel good. People are also drawn to someone who is smiling. You can become a beacon of positive energy by doing something as simple as turning on that smile.

If you don't believe us, you might believe an article from *Psychology Today* from 2012 that stated, "Each time you smile, you throw a little feel-good party in your brain. The act of smiling activates neural messaging that benefits your health and happiness." The author of the article, Ronald E. Riggio, PhD, explained that neurotransmitters, like dopamine, endorphins, and serotonin, are all released when a smile flashes across your face, which not only relaxes your body, but can even lower your heart rate and blood pressure. So, go ahead and smile, be silly if you want. Nothing profound will suddenly change in your life but maybe, just maybe, you will feel more positive about your day ... so go ahead and smile right now.

Now that wasn't so hard?

THE ADVENTURE

As you read through this Guidebook and proceed along your personal Adventure, remember there is no one-size-fits-all approach. Personal Positivity enhances your life, but in different ways for each person. After all, you are unique.

The key to embracing this power is adopting a positive lifestyle that is refreshing in a world in which we are bombarded by negativity. You can be that person with a positive outlook: the one who looks for the silver lining within a situation and understands that being positive is a key to enjoying your life. As you move through this Adventure, remember that it's not just about the great results you will reach—and you will accomplish some great things—it's also very much about the journey. Keep in mind that the journey can be rewarding and bring about exciting changes in your life.

It's not unlike taking a cross-country trip by car or bus. If you travel from New York to San Francisco, you look forward to seeing the Golden

Gate Bridge and Fisherman's Wharf. But the trip can be much more fun if you also stop off at towns and cities along the way to take in sights like Rocky Mountain National Park and Mount Rushmore. A adventure is often exhilarating, and this adventure into Personal Positivity should be no exception.

Rather than taking snapshots of sights and cities, on this Adventure you should take notes, reread sections for clarity, review the recaps at the end of each Guidebook, and do the exercises. You'll also want to check in with yourself to see that you are staying on course, banging away at negative thoughts. This is not a journey to hurry through, it's meant to be traveled slowly so you let the concepts soak in and live them. This is how you will get the most out of your Pozzam Adventure.

WIN TODAY

Each day we are presented with a gift: the gift of time, time in which you can make forward progress in your goals and ambitions, large or small. To do this you need to get out there and attack the day. Get out there and accomplish something that will move you forward in some manner. Decide what you want to accomplish and do what it takes. If you have a report to write for work, an exam to study for in school, new code to write for a software program, a house that needs repairs, whatever it is, do it! You may not finish, but you can make progress.

It's up to you to take on the challenge, to take action and own the day.

When you accomplish what you set out to do, you win the day. And it's a great feeling to be a winner. Winning the day is not a competition against anyone else, nor is it about someone else losing; it's about the positives that occurred in your day. It's about taking on your personal or business challenges and achieving something important to you, that moves you forward. Remember, you won't accomplish large goals and major changes in a day. But each day you challenge yourself to accomplish and take steps forward, you can say, "I've won the day." Look at each day as a contest with yourself and be extremely honest with yourself.

At the end of the day, only you can answer the following questions:

- ☑ Did I focus on what I could do today?
- ☑ Did I have a plan?
- ☑ Did I move the plan forward?
- ☑ Did I take time to focus on me?
- ☑ Did I make progress?
- ☑ Did I take advantage of the precious resource of time to attack the day, and ...
- ☑ *Did I win today?*

EXERCISES

The end of each Guidebook will include exercises that can help you along your adventure. Don't get stressed if an exercise has you stumped—go back to it when you are ready. Remember, the Adventure to Personal Positivity takes time. You need to believe you can do it and that you will get there; you need to embrace the process. You need to own it! But what you don't need to do is wear a Super Hero costume! (unless you want to of course)

EXERCISES FOR GUIDEBOOK 1

DON'T WORRY; THESE EXERCISES DO NOT INVOLVE HEAVY LIFTING.

1 *MAKE A SMALL CHANGE:* As mentioned in the Guidebook, I want you to think about a simple change you would like to make in your daily life, something simple you could do every day. Perhaps you want to learn a new language; you could learn a new word each day and practice it for a little while. Then you could repeat it the next day and learn another new word. The point is, make it simple, write it down, and then find a way to remind yourself.

2 *RECOGNIZE NEGATIVE THINKING:* Challenge yourself to begin the process of noticing when you have a negative thought; learn and recognize how negative thoughts slip into your mind. Make a note in writing, or mentally, when you catch yourself thinking negatively. After you start doing so, you will begin to catch yourself more often. You have to learn how your mind is working to truly control your thoughts.

3 *CREATE A POSITIVE THOUGHT LIST:* To push out negative thoughts with positive ones, have some positive thoughts or sayings at the ready. Make a mental or written list of five things you enjoy thinking about. They could be anything that makes you feel positive. When negativity is clouding your thoughts, you can push them out with the positive thoughts on your list—you can also add to, or change, your list as you think of other positive thoughts.

4 *SMILE:* How many times did you smile today just for the heck of it? How many smiles did you give away? How many smiles did you receive? Keep a rough tally for a day.

5 *WIN TODAY!* At the end of each day challenge yourself. Ask yourself: Did I win today? Did I get the most out of today? Did I move forward/make progress today? Did I use the precious resource of time wisely? Did I give away any smiles? Did I receive any smiles?

CLEAN IT!

SO, WE KNOW THAT PERSONAL POSITIVITY can give you a new attitude and outlook on life. We know that it's not a quick fix, but a step-by-step Adventure that takes time, effort, and consistency, and we know that effort will pay off with a greater sense of fulfillment. But that's just the beginning.

You've learned that you are in control of your daily thought processes—how you think and react to things. You can stop negative thoughts in their tracks, and *you, and you alone* can make the decision to change your life by starting with small steps and building on them over time.

Most importantly, the first Guidebook was all about taking ownership over your thoughts, your attitude, and your life. By embracing the path to Personal Positivity, you own it!

TIME FOR SOME CLEANING

The saying "Out with the old and in with the new" will be the guiding principle for this Guidebook, but this isn't spring cleaning in the traditional sense. Rather, we're looking at cleaning out negativity from your past that still holds you back. No *physical* heavy lifting, but maybe a little *metaphorical* heavy lifting. On the bright side, what you learned in the first

Guidebook has given you the tools to handle that emotional lifting with grace and ease. This is all about clearing the past in order to make space for your new beginning.

CLEANING OUT THE PAST

Getting stuck in the past is easy. It's a common habit that many of us struggle to break out of. We get tied up in things that have already happened and when we try to let go, we find that we're so tangled in it that we're not sure where to start extracting ourselves. But the thing is, the past doesn't need to hold power over your present.

Think of the past like a physical place. Perhaps you grew up in a lovely house with your family, but at some point you moved. You have fond memories of the place, but you cannot live there now. The moment you moved out, you stopped being the person who lives in that house. It's the same thing with your past. Who you are cannot be or change who you were last week, last month, a year, a decade ago. And that's a good thing. There's tremendous power in that. But only if you can break the cycle.

Breaking the cycle is the first step to paving the way toward a fresh, clean slate on which to build your positive mindset and brighter future. How do you break the cycle? First, it's important to stop the blame game. No matter what has happened in your past, it does not deserve the power you give it by placing the blame on it to keep you from moving forward today. Regardless of how you got here, this is where you are. You can't go back, so where do you go from here? This is the defining moment. From here on out, it's up to you to let the past go. To acknowledge that you have that power within you.

You can learn from the past, but there's no reboot or rewind. Time machines just don't exist.

In an early episode of the television sitcom *The Big Bang Theory*, the band of nerdy friends buy a replica of a time machine online and somehow get this giant contraption into their apartment. At first, they enjoy sitting in the time machine and fantasizing about where they could go back to while playing with all the lights and gadgets. But then their neighbor points out the absurdity of four grown men spending hours pretending to go back in time. They recognize that obsessing about living in another time period is pointless—and soon they get rid of the cumbersome device. The point is, none of us can go back in time. We can only live in the present, or in "the now."

The more baggage we accumulate from the past, the more we drag ourselves down. The tighter we cling to negative baggage, the heavier it becomes and the harder it is to move forward. *This is why you never see a race car with a full luggage rack on the roof—it would make it pretty hard to win the race.*

Sometimes our attachment to negative memories can feel like it's protecting us from repeating harmful habits in the future, but in reality the attachment is only keeping us shackled by the feelings associated with that negative memory. It's important to release yourself from the burden of those memories. If it helps, try this visualization: Imagine a large closet filled with old boxes and cartons. Now imagine how much space would be in there if you cleared each and every one of those boxes out. The big, heavy ones; the small, oddly-shaped ones; the ones you can hardly remember why they're there in the first place; the ones you just put in there last week. Mentally take them each out and thank them for protecting you in the wake of something rough, but get rid of them. You don't need them anymore. Now picture yourself filling the closet with new things. Things that bring you joy, things that light you up, things that create the bright, beautiful future you want so badly. That is what this Guidebook is all about. We're clearing out the past to make room for positive thoughts, positive plans, and the experiences that come with your new, positive lifestyle.

We know cleaning out the negatives from the past is not an easy task. Often, getting out of the past to move forward starts with one step forward and two steps back, because the past keeps pulling you back. But, if you remind yourself that the past won't change, and work hard to focus on positive thoughts, you will move forward. The key to this is to start focusing on the present, the now, what's positive about today, where you are right now and what you can do to Win Today. Remind yourself as many times as you need to, over and over again, that you cannot change the past, but you absolutely CAN change today. You can make today positive and productive, you can take steps TODAY to make TOMORROW better.

This isn't to say that getting stuck in the *negative* past is the only thing that can hold you back. Reliving positive moments in your history can keep you from reaching your potential or moving forward to create a positive future, too. Consider the high school football star who is languishing in their career, now. Reliving the glory days won't get them where they need to go in the present.

That being said, psychologically speaking, humans do tend to dwell on the negative more heavily than the positive. Clifford Nass, a professor of communication at Stanford University, says that, "Some people do have a more positive outlook, but almost everyone remembers negative things more strongly and in more detail." He explains the way the brain seems to focus more on the negatives, citing that "negative emotions generally involve more thinking, and the information is processed more thoroughly than positive ones. Thus, we tend to ruminate more about unpleasant events—and use stronger words to describe them than happy ones."

Roy F. Baumeister, a professor of social psychology at Florida State University, adds that losing money, being abandoned by friends, and receiving criticism will have a greater impact than winning money, making friends, or receiving praise. In a research paper he wrote, "You are more upset about losing $50 than you are happy about gaining $50."

Unlocking your Personal Positivity Superpower won't wipe out all negativity. The power here doesn't lie in suddenly becoming impervious to negative events. When bad things happen it will still upset you—and it should! You're human, after all. It just means that when hard times come, you'll be better equipped to handle them. Focusing on positivity also doesn't mean that recounting stories with friends or looking over photos from the past are bad things. Memories are powerful emotional tools and can make us feel connected when we begin to wonder where we belong, or if we belong at all. But harnessing the Power of Positivity reminds us that while a brief visit to the past can be beneficial, ruminating on and trying to set up camp in the past isn't helpful.

So, what can you do to clean out the negatives of your past? Going back to Guidebook 1, you need to start banging away at these thoughts to clean them out of your mind. You need to pull or push yourself back to present time. This is how you start cleaning out the anger, resentment, regrets, hostility, and sadness that hold you back. Is it simple? No—it can be very difficult, but there is a fighter in all of us who can overcome the drag of anything in our pasts.

You can use positive self-talk effectively to help when you find yourself stuck in the past. For example, if you find yourself thinking:

- ☑ *"If I had only done…"*
- ☑ *"Why didn't I say…"*
- ☑ *"I still don't understand why…"*
- ☑ *"I wish I had done A instead of B…"*

You are opening the baggage of the past.

Tell yourself to stop. Be tough on yourself. Yell at yourself if necessary. Remind yourself that the past is over!

This is where you want to switch to positive thinking. If you can't switch quickly enough, focus on where you are in the moment. Look around, take a deep breath, blink your eyes a few times, change positions if you are sitting—do something to snap yourself out of your negative thoughts and into the moment. When you are back in the present, you can then set goals and make plans to move forward into the future. This is where you will need to concentrate more of your attention, on positive action items to move you forward.

FORGIVENESS

We want to mention the importance of forgiveness, especially when it comes to leaving the past behind. There is great power in forgiveness; it frees you from what is often a heavy burden.

Too many people hold on to ill will toward others who have done them wrong and harbor feelings inside. Someone might have let you down, disappointed you, or treated you poorly in the past. They may have lied to you, cheated on you, or even stolen from you. As a result, you hold on to feelings of anger, animosity, or even hatred. You cannot forgive others for whatever it was that happened in the past. The worse the situation, the harder it is to forgive someone. Yet you need to unload such negative feelings to make your own Adventure to Personal Positivity easier.

The toughest part about forgiveness is really meaning it. You can tell someone you forgive them and even shake hands, but if you don't really own it, and mean it, you are not going to improve the situation. Therefore, you need to work on truly forgiving someone, which is a process that begins within yourself.

Before you begin on the process of forgiveness, it's important to understand that forgiveness doesn't mean you are acknowledging that whatever someone did was okay. It wasn't. It also doesn't mean you have to become best buddies. You don't. Forgiveness is not really about them; it's something you're doing for yourself. You should not forgive somebody because someone else tells you to do so, not even us. It won't be genuine, and the negative feelings will come back. You need to feel it inside. You need to recognize that the past will not change but that you can release the negative feelings, from the past, that you are holding on to about this person. Remember, only you control your mind; so, this is something you need to do for yourself.

You could talk with the other person and try to resolve the problem, but this is a risk, since he or she might not want to discuss it at all. This can also potentially make things worse. In many cases, people forgive without even contacting the other person.

When you are ready to forgive, you need to acknowledge what happened and think about who the other person was at that time, and what their needs were. The anger is often associated with the question, "Why did they say or do such a thing to me?" By recognizing that people have needs and go about getting them in many ways, you may understand why this person did whatever they did. Someone may have belittled you to feel better about themselves, or needed money so they took advantage of you, or needed to feel more popular so they dated someone else. Perhaps they borrowed from you and never paid you back because they never had extra cash and were embarrassed to tell you. There are so many possibilities. They may have needed to release their anger or frustration that wasn't even meant for you in the first place.

People don't always go about fulfilling their needs in the most appropriate ways. They can be very hurtful, sometimes intentionally, and often without intention. There are many stories of people who are angry at another, and that other person doesn't even know it.

By recognizing why someone did what they did, you can better understand what happened. You may still react emotionally when you think about it. That's okay. With forgiveness at the forefront of your mind, you can put the negativity to bed even if you have that visceral emotional reaction. You can move forward with positive thoughts.

Like so many other pieces of this adventure, forgiveness may take time, but it's worth the effort. Keep working at it, because the result is freedom for *you*, and that's important. Psychologists and therapists often recommend writing down your thoughts about what happened, why it happened, and how it made you feel. These professionals may even suggest putting it in the form of a letter to the person you are thinking about forgiving. You don't have to *send* the letter. It's simply a method to get the feelings out. Once you've released those emotions, feel free to tear up or even burn (safely) the letter.

Whether you actually say the words "I forgive you" to the other person, or just say them out loud to yourself, it is at that point you are ready to move forward. It is also the point where you can get on with your life and push the situation out of your mind. While it's next to impossible to *actively* forget something, the more you move on with your life, and put the entire matter far behind you, the more likely you are to forget the situation entirely.

PRESENT TIME

Staying in present time is so important. You can only live in the now, not in the past and not in the future.

What's great about living in the present is that you can take positive steps to make changes now. A friend of ours recently lost his job, and it was very painful for him. He kept reliving things that happened at his job and thinking about how he could have changed them. He kept asking what if he had learned a new software program or worked more hours. He was very upset over losing his job, and he had every right to be upset. But in reality, the moment the company told him he no longer worked there, the job was in the past. The more he focused on the job, the more he was living in the past and using negative energy. This is a critical concept you will learn to accept as truth: each moment is its own and when it has happened it is over, done, in the past. You will use this concept constantly in your life, when you accept it, just as our friend came to believe in it.

After a few days of sulking, he immediately started focusing on present time and what he could do now to change his situation. He no longer dwelled on the past. Instead he focused on making the best plans he could for his future. He charted a path to follow step-by-step to start his own business. In time, the business far exceeded the success he had in his old company. Today, he has never been happier and lives each day with an incredible positive mindset. Had he held on to the past and remained angry and bitter over losing his job, he would not have changed his life.

Most successful people endured negative experiences before becoming successful. If they had chosen to hang on to the unpleasant experiences, rather than staying in the present and planning for the future, we might not know their names today. Consider the young athlete who tried out as a sophomore for his high school varsity basketball team but didn't make it. If they carried around that disappointment, rather than working on their game and trying out again the next year, we would never have heard of Michael Jordan. Instead, Jordan put in extra time and worked hard day after day at the gym. He then joined the junior varsity team and after putting up some 40-point games, gained the attention of the varsity coach, who put him on the team the following year.

You might also think about how much animosity you can accumulate by being rejected from film school several times. This could weigh you down, shake your self-confidence, and keep you dwelling on your failed attempts. But if you maintain a positive attitude, get over the rejections, and keep trying, you could become a huge success in the film industry. That's what Steven Spielberg did after multiple rejections to the University of Southern

California School of Cinematic Arts. Rather than sulking about his rejections, Spielberg attended California State University in Long Beach and pursued film on his own, taking an unpaid intern job at Universal Studios doing editing. Determined to break into film, he learned as much as he could and finally made his own short film called *Amblin'*, which won awards and led to his first contract as a director.

Imagine starting your first novel's manuscript, after dreaming of becoming a writer your whole life, on scraps of paper at coffee shops and on delayed trains. Many people would give up on the idea of being a novelist at all. Now imagine losing your mother six months into your writing and never having told her that you were writing the manuscript. Imagine becoming a single mother living off of welfare all while finishing this manuscript. Imagine receiving rejection letter after rejection letter, and still deciding to keep going through it all. That's what J. K. Rowling did. That manuscript was the first *Harry Potter* book. Now, she's the mastermind behind a cultural phenomenon.

None of these incredibly successful people would have ever made their mark on the world if they let the frustration or resentment from failing build inside them. They took a positive attitude, cleaned out the negativity quickly, and refused to let such negativity hold them back. Instead, they focused on the present and planned their future.

LIVING IN THE FUTURE

We've talked about cleaning cobwebs out of the past, but we should also note that in order to stay present, you cannot live in the future, either. The same time machine that won't take you to the past won't let you travel to the future. Setting goals, planning, and considering your next steps is important, yes, but getting caught up in the *idea* of what the future could hold without living and acting in the present moment to make it reality can be as detrimental as getting stuck in the past.

Looking ahead and planning for the future can be great. You can think about what you want to do with your life, your career, your relationships, and new Adventures. If, for example, you want to go from your current position at work to a managerial role, you can plan your ascent. If you are planning to open your own business, there are a ton of things you will need to do before opening day. From a business license, to funding, to finding a location, to staffing, starting a business will take a lot of planning.

We caution you not to obsess about the future. If you start living in the future, you may forget to take care of the now. Often people get so wrapped up in planning ahead—whether it's graduating school or opening a new business—that they no longer focus on present time. There's a story of a restaurant owner who was so excited to open their new restaurant that they spent all their time planning new menu items, expansion, themes for upcoming holidays, and other activities for the future of the restaurant. What they forgot to do was pay attention to the "now" by looking around and seeing that there were not enough customers. They needed to stay in the now and take care of present activities, like hiring good staff, and marketing the restaurant so people would show up, but they were so busy living in the future, and not in present time, that they ran themselves out of business.

The point is, while it's wonderful to set lofty goals and dream about owning a business, or becoming a doctor, lawyer, realtor, aviator, engineer, star athlete, or whatever you choose to do in your future, you can't actually be one until you take the small steps, pass the exams, practice your skills, learn about the industry, and so on. You can dream about your future, and plan for it, but you need to stay rooted in present time as you make your way to all your terrific future plans.

REMEMBER, IT'S AN ADVENTURE

On an Adventure such as this, if you are cleaning out the past, but keep slipping back into negative thoughts about things that happened many years ago, you need to tell yourself this is just a bump in the road, a blip in the process, I'll keep on pressing on and moving forward.

Whether you are on a short journey or a long one, you cannot let each misstep along the way, each detour, or each obstacle stop you. For those of you who play golf, the idea of getting from the tee to the green means taking several shots, the fewer the better. But you may have bunkers, sand traps, water hazards, and other obstacles to navigate over or around before you can get to the green and sink a putt. Let's face it, if golfers gave up every time, they faced an obstacle or landed in a sand trap there would be no one left playing the game.

Our point is simple—don't let anything stop you from staying on your path. Missteps and obstacles are bound to happen. That's life. Life's Adventures are full of highs and lows; this Adventure is no exception. Don't spiral downhill after a misstep; just dust yourself off and keep on going.

CHECK IT!

If you are taking a long drive, you will typically check your gas, check the oil level, and perhaps even check your tire pressure. Most of us also make sure to go to the doctor at least once a year for a checkup. At the gym, after a workout, you might check your time, pace, and distance. Why do we do these things? Because we want to know how we're doing. The same holds true on this journey—you need to check in with yourself along the way.

Checking yourself means seeing how well you are doing along the way. Have you been maintaining the small change you decided to make daily? If you missed a day, did you get back and continue the next day?

Have you been able to push negative thoughts out with positive ones? Remember, you've just started, so give yourself some grace. Sometimes things will trigger negative thinking and set you back a few steps. When these negative thoughts started filling your mind again, were you able to stop them in their tracks and replace them with positive thoughts? If not, don't beat yourself up over it. You may need more practice pushing out the negative thoughts. Remember, you're still very new at this process.

When checking your progress, it's important to be honest. Lying to yourself will only make your journey on this Adventure harder. Check yourself frequently, check yourself honestly, and keep adjusting as necessary.

EMOTIONS

We say it several times in the book: we can't, and shouldn't, ignore our emotions. You have every right to feel the way you do. For one thing, there are lots of positive emotions, like joy, hope, enthusiasm, happiness, contentment, cheerfulness, amusement, and love, to name a few. These emotions are great for us and very positive. The emotions we need to learn how to deal with are the negative ones, like sadness, anger, jealousy, depression, resentment, and hatred.

Having these emotions is also very normal but letting them control us is where we run into trouble.

You have a right to feel your feelings however and whenever they show up—often, these emotional reactions are trying to tell us something about ourselves, the others involved in the situation, or the situation itself. But stewing in the same one without taking stock of why it's part of your current reality or what you might be able to do to move from a negative space to a more positive one is where we do ourselves a disservice.

CONTROLLING EMOTIONS

Emotions are a significant part of life; they are what makes us human. In order to control them to the extent we must in order to maintain control over our lives, we have to acknowledge them as they come along. Consider the last time you saw someone shouting something like "I'M NOT ANGRY!" while throwing their hands in the air or going red in the face. That's not exactly the healthy relationship with your emotions we're going for.

A great starting place for getting a handle on your emotions is better understanding the situations that make you emotional. Get to know your "hot spots," or emotional triggers, and try to change those situations. If you know you get very angry every day when you're running late for work, and traffic or some last-minute chore slows you down, you could plan your day to start earlier. Give yourself more time to get to work so you will be less likely to get angry. If you get frightened speaking in public at meetings or speaking engagements, you could practice what you will be speaking about with your friends, rehearse, use index cards with notes, and limit the time in which you will be speaking. Preparation and being proactive make speaking easier even for the many people who fear it. Again, if you know when you are likely to experience negative emotions, you can be proactive and minimize the emotional reaction.

Your goal is to be able to control your emotions rather than having them control you. As we proceed through the Pozzam Adventure we will talk more about emotions in the upcoming Guidebooks. We will learn more positive ways of reacting to negative emotions, methods of controlling them, and how to channel and transform your feelings into other, more positive responses. We will learn how to turn disappointment to passion and drive, anger to excitement, sadness into a mission, and so forth. For now, however, it's important to understand that emotions are part of being human. By acknowledging them and taking basic steps to control what triggers the negative ones, you can start controlling them.

EXERCISES FOR GUIDEBOOK 2

1 Think about people, situations, or events in your past that you blame for where you are today, your present circumstances. Write them down. Look at the list, then burn the list.

2 Write down the name of anyone you hold a grudge against, or you believe has done you wrong. Look at the names, think about them, look deep down inside yourself, now remind yourself that they are not relevant to your life today, and there is no reason to let them take up your mental energy. Then forgive them. You don't need to call or meet them—just say to yourself that you truly forgive them, then make like Elsa and let it go!

3 Check in with yourself, be in the present. What is happening today? What is in front of you? What is going on around you? Did you do your small change activity today?

4 Write down some things that trigger negative emotions for you, things that always get you angry or upset you. Now plan and write down three steps to avoid them.

5 *WIN TODAY!* At the end of each day challenge yourself. Ask yourself: Did I win today? Did I get the most out of today? Did I move forward/make progress today? Did I use the precious resource of time wisely? Did I give away any smiles? Did I receive any smiles?

ACCEPT IT!

IN THE LAST GUIDEBOOK we talked about the need to clean out negative thoughts from the past that take you out of present time and slow you down when you try to move forward. We also discussed the power of forgiveness and how forgiving can free you from a heavy burden. Then, we focused on the importance of living in present time and introduced the significance of emotions and the role they play in our lives. Now, in this Guidebook, we want to introduce the concept of acceptance and openness.

ACCEPTANCE AND OPENNESS

According to the dictionary definition, to accept is to be ready to receive, take something in, agree to a suggestion, believe something is right, true, or real.

Openness refers to an individual's personal level of acceptance and conscious awareness of the possibility that change may be needed across a range of situations and scenarios. It's considered a personality trait; for some it is innate and for others it can be learned. Someone who is open is driven to enact change. They have an accommodating attitude and are receptive to new ideas, behaviors, cultures, people, environments, and experiences. Their attitude and opinions typically come from a broad spectrum of ideas that differ from that which are more familiar, conventional, or traditional.

An individual who enjoys experiencing new things is someone with a high level of openness. Such people are typically curious, imaginative, creative, flexible, adventurous, and open-minded.

Openness therefore seems to be a precursor to acceptance, because it's very difficult to accept something new if you are not open to receiving it.

ARE YOU OPEN TO CHANGE?

Now that we have defined openness, we want to challenge you with some important questions:

- ☑ Are you open to change?
- ☑ Do you agree something has to change in your life now?
- ☑ If you agree, are you ready to make such a change happen?
- ☑ Do you have the drive, and a real burning desire, to bring about that change?

If you answer *yes* to these questions, you recognize that openness leads to a conscious awareness that change is necessary. You are also ready and willing to make that change. This means it's time make an action plan to bring about that change.

Ask yourself:

- ☑ What can I do to bring about change?
- ☑ What do I need that I do not yet have?
- ☑ Who do I need to meet that can be of help?
- ☑ What information do I need to learn?

You'll find your answers to these questions by turning to the attributes that accompany openness. In fact, you'll see how living with openness plays out in our everyday lives. Consider **curiosity**, which is defined as a strong desire to learn or to know something new. This means being an explorer, or even a detective, asking questions, and constantly wanting to learn more. Taking courses, researching your areas of interest, and learning as much as you can about the change you are looking to make all stem from being curious and wanting greater knowledge.

Think about what it is to be **imaginative** and dream about all sorts of new and even uncharted possibilities. Creativity and inventiveness come from imagining new and different ways of doing things. The greatest inventors and innovators have tapped into their imagination and reshaped the world. Consider Mark Zuckerberg, Elon Musk, Marie Curie, Grace Hopper, and Dr. Shirley Jackson, to name a few. Imagination also sparks the creativity of great designers, decorators, architects, and artists. Letting your imagination flow freely gives you the opportunity to look at things in a new and different way, which can help you make changes.

Openness also means being **adventurous** and trying new things and new experiences. As Nike has been saying for years, "Just Do It." It's really not a bad philosophy. Trying something new can be motivating; it can get you out of a rut, away from negativity, and energize you. Consider the 50-year-old who tried skydiving for the first time, the 65-year-old who learned to ski, the 30-year-old who volunteered at the Special Olympics for the first time, the shy young person who got on stage at a comedy club and did stand-up comedy, the inventor who took their brand-new business idea to *Shark Tank*, or the business owner who was open to trying a new type of advertising to build the company brand. Adventure recharges your battery, keeps you interested and excited about life.

If you are going to realize the full power of Personal Positivity, openness is crucial. It will lead to incredible discoveries about yourself and about the world around you. It will also lead to great changes in your life.

OPEN-MINDEDNESS

Openness also includes being open-minded, which is defined as being willing to listen to other people and consider new ideas, suggestions, and opinions.

Psychologists point out that you can identify people who have a strong sense of openness in their personality by how they act and communicate. Open-minded people put ideas out there and are open to feedback and input, while closed-minded people do not like anyone challenging their ideas. Open-minded people want to learn from others, so they ask questions. Closed-minded people want things done their way, period. Open-minded people are interested in hearing what you have to say; closed-minded people are interested in what they have to say. You get the idea. When someone says, "It's my way or no way," they are being closed-minded. When someone asks, "Any suggestions?" they are being open-minded.

When people make decisions without being open and are not curious enough to seek out new information, they often miss out on positive possibilities. Consider Mary-Anne, a young actress from years ago who simply refused to believe that anyone would go to see a musical based on poems about cats. "Who's going to want to see that?" she asked her friends. Rather than being open to the idea, and saying, "What the heck, I should go on the audition ... you never know," she decided it was never going to be a hit show. As it turned out *Cats* became one of Broadway's all-time biggest hits. Had Mary-Anne been open-minded and looked up the success of *Cats* in Great Britain she might have gone on that audition, and who knows what might have happened. She let a golden opportunity pass her by because she was closed to it.

In business, being closed-minded limits progress. When someone says, "But we've always done it that way," they are not accepting the possibility of change or progress. They are also not going to move forward and grow.

A story of being closed to innovation in small business comes from a small, family-owned hotel in northern California. For years the hotel did fine, with guests coming to visit the wine country. However, as times changed and technology exploded, the owners couldn't accept the idea that such technology could grow their business. They both refused to listen to their grown children who tried repeatedly to persuade them to digitally market the hotel and take online reservations. As they continued to ignore the growth of on-line marketing, they watched as competitive hotels in the area posted no vacancy signs. Meanwhile, their little hotel had plenty of available rooms. As the hotel's struggles grew, the children took it upon themselves to build a marketing and social media campaign online. When sales began to pick up and their parents were no longer panicking about losing the hotel entirely, the parents came to their children and thanked them for opening their minds and dragging them into the future. This was a case in which not being open to exploring new ideas *almost sunk* the family business.

Of course, being open does not mean you must be open to accepting every idea that comes your way or saying yes to everything—they tested that theory and it didn't work out so well for Jim Carrey in the 2008 film *Yes Man*. Being open to ideas doesn't mean you have to agree with them. However, when you're open to hearing new ideas, and thinking about them, you are more likely to find some exciting possibilities to explore and learn more about. While you don't have to say yes to everything, I bet you could say yes more often. Try it!

You can also be open to personal interaction, which means being willing to interact with other people, rather than saying, "I'm not interested," or "I'm too busy," and closing the door to such possibilities or potential opportunities.

A colleague of ours was telling us that an old friend he hadn't seen in years contacted him about getting together to have a drink. At first, he was going to tell his old buddy that he was busy or make up an excuse for not getting together. Instead, he thought, "Why not?" It was either go out and meet his friend or spend another night at home watching TV. So he met his friend at a nearby pub, had a couple of beers, ordered some food, talked for two hours, and had a great time. Now, he says, they may even have an opportunity to do business together. Even in an era of using technology to avoid person-to-person communication, there is still great value in letting people into your life.

Being open-minded also means accepting people who differ from you or your family. Relationships are often strained, or destroyed, because of closed-mindedness. Consider how many books and movies are centered on closed-mindedness. The story has been told over and over again: Two people who want to be together but one, or both, sets of parents (as well as friends) oppose the relationship. Perhaps, if the Capulets and the Montagues weren't closed-minded, Romeo and Juliet might have lived happily ever after.

Being open to interacting with, and accepting, other people is important. They often have information that benefits you, can provide help, offer feedback to your ideas, and lend support you didn't even know you needed.

ACCEPT

Think of the definition we used at the top of this Guidebook; to accept means to be ready to receive, take something in, agree to a suggestion, and believe something is right, true, or real. Let's add some additional items to that list. Accepting also means that you stop resisting, and you say yes to *more* things.

Do you see how openness and accepting are closely aligned? Once you have recognized openness and embraced it, you can then truly believe in something and accept that the changes you want, you need. This comes through the Superpower of Personal Positivity.

A couple of friends, who were working together, show how Personal Positivity has worked for those who are open to accepting it. Pamela and Rich were in a similar place in their lives; neither was happy with their personal relationships or with their work. They both carried a lot of negative baggage and clearly needed a new outlook and a new plan.

Pamela began learning about the concept of Personal Positivity. She was immediately very open and accepting and quickly embraced the concept, which she recognized would set her on a great path and help her achieve what she really desired in life. Pamela had the courage and drive to make important changes in her life. She took classes and took webinars to improve her status in the workplace. She also started having more open conversations with people closest to her and became better at expressing herself and learned more about her feelings and opinions. Pamela utilized her positive attitude about her own life and the results were amazing. Over the next several months, Pamela planned her future and took the necessary steps to reach her business and Personal goals. Today, Pamela is an executive, is happily married with three wonderful children and has some very special friends. Pamela credits her success to the skills she learned from Personal Positivity.

Rich, on the other hand, remained closed to the idea of Personal Positivity. He did not believe it would help him achieve what he really wanted in life. As a result, he held on to a lot of negativity and did not improve his work or personal life. After recognizing that others around him, including his friend Pamela, were moving up the ladder at work, he began to recognize that something was holding him back—negativity. He had a bad attitude about life being unfair, no matter what you do, which came from friends, family, and previous experiences in his past.

The good news is that Rich gave Personal Positivity another chance. He saw the difference it had made in Pamela's life. Rich has finally started on the Adventure to Personal Positivity and although he is not totally where he wants to be yet, he continues to follow the path today.

Clearly, you are at the threshold of Personal Positivity right now. You were open to this Adventure and you're here, all the way on the third Guidebook. The question is, are you ready to accept what a life of Personal Positivity can bring you? Remember, if you truly accept and embrace Personal Positivity, you will free yourself from all that is holding you back, and as a result you will be able to make significant life changes and reach your goals.

But you must also keep in mind that the word "accept" is a verb; it is not a passive thing. You can't just sit by and expect things to automatically change. Acceptance is an active process and requires effort. As you continue reading and visit the Pozzam.com website, we will train you to set your goals and work toward those goals. It will take work on your part; roadblocks and adversity will come your way. But having truly accepted the path of Personal Positivity, you will be guided to doing what is right for you.

As you proceed along your Adventure to Personal Positivity, you learn to open your eyes, your ears, and your mind to opportunities you may not have recognized before because negativity shielded them from you.

It is crucial to remember that no one decides what you think but you. That means it is you, and only you, that must accept the idea that the power of Personal Positivity can, and will, allow you to make the changes that you want, need, and desire in your life.

ASSUMPTIONS AND PROJECTING THE FUTURE

There's an old joke, from the pre-cell phone era, about a young person whose car stalls at night on a quiet mountain road. Not knowing how to fix the car, they starts walking up the road in hopes of finding someone who can help him. After walking about a half mile, they sees lights in a large house higher up the mountain road. As they trudge up the hill and get closer to the house, they realize how big it really is; even at night, they can see the sprawling grounds. The young person starts thinking, "When I get there, whoever opens the door is going to take one look at me and think I'm some lowlife, or even a criminal. They're going to be skeptical, critical, and laugh at me. They won't help me one bit because they're so much better than me. They're so important and I'm not! Why are they so unfeeling? What's wrong with them? Why are they so arrogant?" As they walk, they get angrier and angrier. Finally, they reach the front gate, open it, storm up the path to the house, and knock on the door. A kindly old gentleman, with a sparkle in his eyes, opens the door, and the young person shouts, "I wouldn't take your help now if you paid me!" And with that, they storm off.

This is what happens when we start making assumptions and projecting what is going to happen. This attitude is very familiar territory for most people. We get all worked up about things, based on nothing but our own imagination, and we start projecting the future.

If your boss asks you to come in for a private meeting in the morning, but that's all you know, it's very easy to start thinking that you are in trouble. You start asking: What will you do about a job? How will you support your family? Where can you start looking for a new job? Then you find that, after you've stayed up all night worrying, all he wanted to discuss was whether you had time available to help with a company project. Of course, you are relieved and say yes, even though you are also now too exhausted to start the project.

Thanks to technology we do this kind of projecting all the time. Since we are living in the age of texting, we often find ourselves staring at a text trying to understand what someone means. Texting is nothing more than words on a screen, we don't always know how the message is intended. Is the other person being sarcastic? Funny? Nasty? So often we read the text and decide how it was intended with absolutely no knowledge of the truth. When someone doesn't text us back, we do the same thing, we project all kinds of reasons we believe they aren't texting us back, but we really don't know.

Unless you have facts or information that points, solidly, to a specific scenario, you're much better off if you leave your assumptions and projections at the door. It's a waste of time and mental energy to do otherwise. If you're feeling uncertain, check the facts and get the information you need to stop projecting.

Studies show that assumptions are largely the reason why people are afraid of public speaking. According to *Psychology Today*, approximately 25 percent of people report experiencing such a fear, which even has a name: *glossophobia*. Unlike the fear of dangerous activities like skydiving, fear of speaking is usually based on people making assumptions that the audience won't find them interesting, won't like what they have to say, or won't like how they sound or look. Before they open their mouths to speak, they have projected a disaster. You could project the speaking engagement as being a big hit, with everyone standing and cheering, but most people, based on their own insecurities, are prone to negative thinking. Either way, you are postulating what will happen.

This is why you need to separate fact from fiction. You need to focus your energy on what is really happening. By acquiring facts and knowledge you can walk into a situation with a better idea of how it will turn out. For this reason, successful public speakers take time to learn about their topic, know their demographics, plan out what they are going to say, know how long they will be speaking, and practice before they step up to the podium.

They take a positive approach and plan rather than assuming or projecting the outcome.

It's also important not to allow yourself to be led down a path by other people's assumptions, or something that you read online. How many people go to WebMD because they have a minor headache and after two minutes on the website are suddenly convinced that they have a brain aneurysm? It's a common trap, but it's one that leads to panic instead of reasonable thought processes.

Living in the real world also requires being honest with yourself about your hopes and dreams. Many people project positive things that are completely unrealistic. Someone who sees himself losing 25 pounds in the next week is not only projecting, but lying to himself, just like someone who believes they are going to open a business in a week or build a house in three days. It's important you remain honest and practical with yourself. Our friend used to joke that he had just signed a contract to play for the Chicago Bulls; only problem was he couldn't get them to sign it.

Dreaming big isn't a bad thing, but it's important to draw the line between a big, achievable dream and what is fantasy, daydream, or unrealistic thinking. Achieving realistic goals requires that we choose a realistic dream and break it down into realistic steps.

ASK YOURSELF: WHY? FINDING YOUR CORE MOTIVATOR

After you accept Personal Positivity into your life you can move forward. But in order to make any real progress, you need to know your core motivator, which isn't *what* you want, but *why* you want it. That is, why are you pursuing these goals and aspirations?

Many people want to start a business, but what keeps them going through the early years of working 50-hour weeks with little, if any, pay to show for their efforts? It's their driving force. Without a driving force, you will lack the passion and enthusiasm to reach your goals or make major changes in your life. So, the question remains. It's not "What do you want to do?" but "Why do you want to do it?"

The knee-jerk reaction for many is financial gain. After all, we live in a world where money talks—and it talks loudly. It's easy to say money is your driving factor, but that's typically not all that's at play. Why do you want money? What about being in a better position financially is most attractive to you? Some entrepreneurs want to have a business to hand down to their children. Others want to bring their new creations or products to the market. Some want to run a company that will benefit the environment or bring affordable medical technology to hospitals and patients in need. Even people who insist that it's all about making money typically have a deeper incentive, such as wanting to enjoy a better life than they had growing up and to give their family what they didn't have.

If you recall, in the first Guidebook, we talked about Denise, a young woman who was determined to become a real estate agent. Her driving force was the need to take care of her two sons. Many people are driven to succeed for those who mean the most to them in life, those for whom they are responsible, whether it's young children or aging parents.

For others it may be a personal goal of independence. Most entrepreneurs are motivated to go into business because they know they have skill sets and abilities that they do not get to use at their current jobs. They want independence, autonomy, and an opportunity to put their stamp on a business that they are passionate about. This explains why, every year, millions of people leave their jobs to strike out on their own.

Gary, from the Midwest, had worked in several businesses, for bosses that were not appreciative of his skills. He was a young inventor, and he took it upon himself to start his own company using his knowledge of nautical technology. He was determined to create new tools that would benefit the ship-building industry, an industry he knew very well. Gary worked long hours for years, along with a partner. From meager beginnings, working in his garage, they eventually landed contracts with major ship builders. The company grew from six people to 600, and eventually—after 20 years—Gary and his partner sold the company for over $100 million.

Creative individuals often find that they want to focus on their skills and showcase their talents in design, fashion, art, music, theater, or another creative outlet. Artists and performers have often said that this is what they were born to do. Their "why" is simple; it's to master their skills. They know they have greatness to offer and want to share their abilities no matter what.

It's okay if you are driven to do something strictly for yourself, such as run in a major marathon. Many are there not because they think they will win, but because of the personal challenge. Others are there for a variety of reasons, such as being motivated to raise money to help other people. For example, over 9,300 runners ran for charity in the 2017 New York Marathon raising over $35 million.

When thinking about your core motivator, keep in mind that it cannot be about doing something that someone else insists you do, nor is it about getting back at someone. A healthy, positive motivator is not "to get back at my boss," or "to teach my ex-girlfriend a lesson." These are simply ways of getting revenge, and revenge doesn't elevate your life in the slightest.

It can be argued that your "why" should not be about beating your competition, but instead about doing the best that you can do. Former Olympic skier (2002 and 2006) Jeremy Bloom, who later became a successful corporate CEO, once explained that when he was skiing and felt motivated solely to beat someone else (external motivation) he did not ski as well as he did when he reached down deep and felt his real core motivation, which was doing the absolute best he could do (internal motivation) without focusing on the competition.

One last note on core motivators; this driving force will likely change over time. What drives you forward at one stage of life may not be the same later on. For example, a young student may be studying hard because they want to get into a good college. Why? Because they want to be an architect, an attorney, or an engineer. Later in life, however, that core driver for an older student may be to support a family.

A former business partner of ours was driven to work hard to support her family. But that motivator changed after nearly 25 years. When her three boys had grown up, she left her job, and became determined to add another Guidebook to her life. She was still young and had a tremendous passion to fight the overwhelming negativity in the world. She started coaching people and running classes on Positivity. Her desire to introduce Personal Positivity to as many people as possible became her driving force. As a result, every time she faced a roadblock, or someone tried to divert her, or minimize her role in helping other people become more positive, she would go back to her core belief and get back on the path with even more passion to move forward. Therefore, her core motivator today is helping people accept and change their lives through the power of their own mind.

OVERCOMING ROADBLOCKS AND SETBACKS

It is very rare, perhaps impossible, to find a success story without road-blocks or setbacks along the way. Studies have shown that people who have faced some obstacles and roadblocks increase their chances of success. A 2010 study from researchers at the University of Buffalo confirms that we fare better after some life difficulties than if we've had many or none at all. The study, called "Whatever Does Not Kill Us," included 2,398 subjects who were assessed repeatedly from 2001 to 2004. The researchers found that those who had experienced some adverse events reported better mental health and well-being than people with a high history of adversity or those with no history of adversity at all.

This is why your core motivation is so important. Each time you face a challenge or obstacle you can go back to that base belief and core driver to propel you forward as it has in other adverse situations.

British inventor Sir James Dyson gives us a story of extreme determination and resilience against many roadblocks. Dyson is the founder of Great Britain's Dyson Ltd., a vacuum cleaner company that today boasts profits of over two billion pounds annually. Dyson's core motivator was his innate ability and passion for taking products, making them better, and selling them to the world. In 1978, Dyson, who had already enjoyed some success with earlier inventions, became so fed up with Hoover vacuum cleaners that when he came across the idea for a bagless vacuum, he became obsessed with the concept of creating one and bringing it to the world. When he set about this task, he could not get the device to work. Dyson started reworking his invention, learning from each failed attempt, while dipping back down to his core motivator repeatedly to keep on moving forward.

After five years, and 5,127 prototypes, Dyson finally got it right. But, when he tried to license his invention and take it to market, he ran into many obstacles, from price issues to disinterest by various companies. He now had the product but had no one to buy it. But he was not deterred. He travelled to Japan where he was finally able to sell what he called the bagless G-Force vacuum, with great success. He later returned to England, started his own business, Dyson Ltd., and outsold the companies that had initially refused to license the product. The rest is business history.

Dyson took a positive attitude to the extreme. He overcame roadblock after roadblock and refused to give up. He has been quoted as saying, "Enjoy failure and learn from it." Of course, you can only do this with an open mind, a core motivator to keep you going, and a positive attitude.

Just like Dyson, you will face challenges and roadblocks. People will get in your way and tell you to give up on your Adventure, but you need to think back on why you are following your path and keep moving forward.

YOUR ADVENTURE

It is important throughout the Adventure to discuss your progress. It will not be a straight line or a smooth ride, but it can be gratifying. You will face adversity, frustration, and sadness as you navigate roadblocks and detours. You will get angry and have negative thoughts. Through this process you will learn how to deal with all those emotional responses and how to own and manage your reactions. You are on your way now and need to keep moving forward, by the Power of You.

EXERCISES FOR GUIDEBOOK 3

1 Do something, anything, that you have never done that is positive and expands your knowledge. Say yes to something you normally wouldn't, accept or offer an invitation to do something you normally would pass on, go to a movie you would never see, accept a project at work you might otherwise turn down, or perhaps go to a meeting of an organization that interests you.

2 Can you think of an example where you projected what you thought was going to happen or assumed someone was thinking or doing something and none of it turned out the way you thought? The next time recognize it and challenge yourself!!

3 Say yes to Personal Positivity, say yes to developing your Superpower, say out loud "I am open to Personal Positivity in my life" and "I am Personally committed to living a life with Positivity so that I may be the best version of me."

4 Tell yourself WHY? You are pursuing a goal, what is your core motivator? What is your why? At your core why do you want to change? Why do you want to be a better you? Why are you willing to put in the work? Dig down deep ... now write it down; this is incredibly important as you will come back to this through the rest of the process.

5 *WIN TODAY!* At the end of each day challenge yourself. Ask yourself: Did I win today? Did I get the most out of today? Did I move forward/make progress today? Did I use the precious resource of time wisely? Did I give away any smiles? Did I receive any smiles?

POZZAM!

ADVENTURE GUIDEBOOK #4

ACT IT!

IN THE PREVIOUS GUIDEBOOK, we talked about the importance of being accepting of, and open to, new ideas, new people, new environments, and making changes. In addition, we discussed the time-wasting process of making assumptions based on no facts and then using such assumptions to project into the future. And finally, we introduced the need to understand not just what you want to change in your life, but *why* you want to make such a change, and identified our core motivator. Now we move from mind to body as we go from thinking to acting.

ACT IT!

Now that you understand Personal Positivity, have taken ownership, cleaned out the baggage of the past, and know why you want to make changes, you need to bring Positivity into your actions. In short, this means it's time to ramp up everything you do and do it with energy and enthusiasm.

We have to do so many things in a given day, so why not get behind them? Why not approach everything with conviction and make a personal promise that you will not allow yourself to have a bad day? Remember, you want to Win the Day, and doing everything with energy and enthusiasm is a winning formula.

Dale Carnegie often talked about the "90-10 Rule," explaining that people are typically fine with 90 percent of the stuff they do in life. It's the other 10 percent that is drudgery. This is where energy and enthusiasm will help the most: to propel you through the unpleasant tasks you encounter. Carnegie said that with the 10 percent you should act "as if" it was one of the things you loved doing.

As kids, most of us had to through things we didn't want to do, usually taking much longer than necessary to complete the task. When we're children, it's harder to muster the energy and enthusiasm for something we don't enjoy. We don't see the bigger picture. However, when we go to college, take classes as an adult, or tackle tasks that we don't enjoy, it gets easier to do the work because we choose classes we enjoy and approach such classes with energy, enthusiasm, and a Positive attitude.

When you're doing something you love, there's a natural flow, a spark that makes propelling yourself with that energy and enthusiasm so much easier. Imagine being able to take that spark and apply it to everything in your day. You would get through things more quickly, more efficiently, and feel better about each thing you accomplish. Each part of your day is a piece of a larger puzzle, a step toward achieving your goals. Keeping that in mind infuses a sense of purpose and Positivity into everything you do.

People tend not to think about the positive results of getting things accomplished. They whine and complain about the less interesting tasks in front of them, and either look for ways to get out of them or come up with excuses not to do them. However, it is found that completing tasks, especially those related to goals, is beneficial. In a *Psychology Today* article called "Goal Progress and Happiness," Timothy A. Pychyl, PhD, points out that "to the extent that we're making progress on our goals, we're happier emotionally and more satisfied with our lives."

Scientists have noted on numerous occasions that accomplishing even small tasks leaves people feeling good, thanks to the release of dopamine, which explains why people feel a sense of accomplishment when completing a task. In some cases, there's also a sense of relief or satisfaction. It stands to reason that most people would want more of these good feelings!

Now, you're probably asking yourself how in the world you're going to muster up enthusiasm and energy for things like taking out the garbage, doing your taxes, folding the laundry, or clearing out your inbox? We promise, it's doable!

You could focus your mind on something more fun, or you can find outside stimulation. A friend of ours was telling us that he and his wife both get home at the same time from work, so they split up the chores. One of his weekly chores is to clean the kitchen and wash the floor. Not a fun chore, but he sees it as a great opportunity to listen to Bruno Mars. So, he mops to the music of Bruno and has fun doing a less-than-exciting chore. And today with so many voice-controlled devices at the ready, you can easily program what you want to hear, from a book on tape to a baseball game to Michael Bublé. You could also reverse the process: instead of listening to music, sing. A guy we know sings *You Are So Beautiful* while cleaning his kitchen. He claims it inspires him to "make the kitchen look beautiful."

Another great way to make chores enjoyable is to make them into games. Can you break your own speed record? How quickly can you unload the dishwasher without breaking anything?

You can also exercise while doing chores. Count your lunges while vacuuming, or jog to and from the store, provided you're not carrying too many bags back home. Then count your lifts while putting things up into the cabinets or in the closet.

Another effective tactic is rewarding for yourself. If you're pushing through unpleasant paperwork in the office, treat yourself to your favorite local spot for lunch, or promise yourself a certain span of time to spend on something you love when you get home. Decide you can watch your favorite movie or finally catch up on that show you've missed the last few weeks of. Whatever it takes to generate some enthusiasm, do it!

Your day will, inevitably, include some drudgery. The point here is, if you can apply some creativity, you can inspire yourself to get through that. If we act "as if" then maybe, in time, what used to feel like drudgery no longer does. This isn't to say there won't be unpleasant tasks in life. But when you get into the habit of approaching everything you do with energy and enthusiasm; those two modes of operating become a way of life.

In life, it's all about how you "show up," whether at work or in social situations. One person gets excited and tackles the task at hand, while another person mopes, lingers, doesn't display any energy, and clearly doesn't really "show up," even if he or she is physically standing there.

Have you ever noticed how people act when they are introduced to someone new? One person will smile, make eye contact, say "nice to meet you" (perhaps include the new name), and reach out with a firm handshake. Others will just nod, say "hi" or something under their breath, and their handshake will be like grabbing hold of a wet fish. The difference is that one person exemplifies energy and enthusiasm, while the other approaches meeting someone new as an unpleasant task or a chore. This begs the question, in either a business or a social situation, which of these people would you want to talk with and possibly get to know better? The one who gave you a positive greeting or the one who didn't seem to care about meeting you in the slightest?

It's interesting in a well-balanced work environment to look around the room when a new assignment is handed out. If you watch the reactions of the staff, you'll see that some people immediately get into the project and start asking questions and exploring how to go about completing the task, while others immediately take a negative attitude about how long it will take and how much work it will be to get through the assignment. Which person do you think others want on their team? And who will ultimately be trusted and given more responsibility by their boss?

When you "act it" you are illustrating to yourself, as well as to others, that you are living with Personal Positivity. This will always open you up to many more opportunities and possibilities.

PROCRASTINATION

Procrastination is defined as intentionally putting off the doing of something that should be done.

It is the enemy of accomplishment. Procrastination is like an evil little villain lurking around the corner just waiting until you are ready to get started on a task or an activity. It wants to lure you away with tons of excuses *not* to get to it. The arguments for procrastination are that you can always do it later, or tomorrow, or the day after that, or that you might enjoy taking a nap or having a snack, mindlessly watching television, or perusing the web.

You must not let procrastination win the battle. Clearly the best time to start fighting procrastination is now, because if you wait around ... the evil villain wins the day.

Pamela Wiegartz, PhD, and co-author of the book *The Worrier's Guide to Overcoming Procrastination: Breaking Free from the Anxiety that Holds You Back,* points out that procrastination becomes a pattern that repeats itself. This is a result of people being told, or telling themselves, that they are "disorganized, lazy, or worse, because they just don't care enough!" She also adds that "most of the time, nothing could be further from the truth. Procrastinators are often smart, capable, hardworking people—they just can't get things done on time and can't seem to figure out why."

One reason people procrastinate is based in that negativity we are working to battle here. Negativity creeps in as a result of negative self-talk and negative messages received over and over, making it difficult to see your personal path to success. If this sounds familiar, it's time to lean on the tools we developed a couple Guidebooks ago and clear out those negative thoughts and associations. Letting the past go and choosing to forge ahead to a future without the shackles of those self-limiting beliefs is a must-do if you want to kiss procrastination goodbye.

Best friends Claudia and Loretta were both excellent undergraduate students at a major university. They had grown up together, travelled together, and studied together, working hard to achieve the necessary grades to get accepted into law school. However, the schools that accepted them were a few thousand miles apart, and over time, their approaches to law school changed. Claudia continued to work hard, guided by her passion and desire, to become an environmental lawyer and make a difference in the world. She embraced and accepted Personal Positivity in her life; when she hit difficult times, she pushed through them, not allowing negativity or procrastination to slow her down.

Loretta, however, found herself having a hard time in law school. For her, schoolwork had always come easily. Now, rather than fighting through tough classes, studying harder, or joining study groups, she began putting off studying, hanging out more with friends off campus, and finding many ways to procrastinate. She got lazy and had not cleaned out her negatives or taken positive steps to complete law school. Ultimately, this led to her downfall. She left law school and took some office jobs while trying to figure out what to do with her life.

The problem for Loretta was that she did not have a core motivator, so without one, she got easily distracted, and procrastination took over. After a few years, she realized that her core motivator had been following Claudia to law school, not an innate desire to become a lawyer herself.

Shortly after this, she started exploring a path to Personal Positivity, which encouraged her to think about what really mattered to her, what could drive her. She realized that her passion was education, and that she really wanted to teach. This time Loretta acted on her own personal goal, and her enthusiasm fueled her to go back to school for a teaching degree. She's been a high school business law teacher for a dozen years, and still keeps in touch with her friend Claudia, who is now a partner in a law firm in Minnesota. They are both happy with the way things worked out and are doing what they really wanted to do.

So why do we procrastinate and how do we fight it? First, we procrastinate because we don't know, or have forgotten, our "why." If you're not sure why you are working toward something, it's very easy to become a procrastinator. Loretta didn't know why she wanted to be a lawyer, so she was not motivated to work hard to achieve her goal ... which was really her friend's goal.

Sir Isaac Newton said that a body at rest will stay at rest until compelled to do otherwise. He was referring to physics, but it applies here as well. You need to use your "why" as a compelling force to generate the energy and enthusiasm that will propel you into action. Nobody is going to do this for you. Only you can decide why you want to do something, what you are going to do, and when you are going to do it—so if you decide you're going to sit on the couch today, and do nothing, that is your choice. If you are going to head over to the gym and exercise to get into better shape, or lose weight, that is also your choice.

Another factor that contributes to procrastination is the feeling of overwhelm. When a task, project, activity, or situation feels overwhelming, it's easy to put it off. It's easy to say the task is too difficult or will take too long. It's easy to be negative about it. But the power to break that task down into smaller tasks and chunks that aren't overwhelming, that you can wrap your head around, is in your hands. You have the ability to empower yourself by "chunking." Take writing a book, for example. The idea of drafting a manuscript is enormous. But if you break it down into chunks—an outline, Guidebooks, scenes—it becomes much more manageable. Many larger tasks that at first appear overwhelming become more manageable by chunking. There is an old saying, by Lao Tzu, that every journey starts with the first step; this means that each task you complete, each accomplishment you achieve, all started with you going and doing something. So, let's get going!

Procrastination can also be spurred by the assumption of a negative outcome, external pressure, negative messages coming from those around you, or a lack of support. There are a number of things that make procrastination, which is already an easy choice, even easier to make. So how the heck are you supposed to fight that?

Many people fight off procrastination by creating, and holding themselves accountable for following, a schedule. If you're going to the gym before work, make sure it's on the schedule, along with your business appointments and social plans. Then you need to self-talk your way through—you can even self-nag or self-badger yourself a little to stick to your schedule. Sure, you'll go off schedule at some point, but the more you push yourself to stick with it, the easier it will get to fight procrastination and accomplish things. You also need to fight your way through procrastination with reminders of your "why" and a positive attitude that includes approaching everything you do with energy and enthusiasm.

THE ONLY WAY THROUGH IT IS THROUGH IT

If you've ever sat down to do your taxes and taken a long pause, as most of us do, before getting started, you'll know what we mean when we say "the only way through it is through it". You don't want to do your taxes, but you must, and so you will.

In life, at some point you may face more distressing or overwhelming situations than tax returns, such as cleaning up after a fire or if disaster strikes your home or business. You may have to get through a very tough personal situation, like a long-drawn-out divorce complete with lawyer visits and emotional meetings with your ex, or a business venture going south where you're forced to shut down the company. This means doing a lot of work that may be unpleasant but still needs to get done. You have no other choice. There are debts to pay, leases to negotiate, and employees to deal with, not to mention clearing out, or selling off, equipment and furniture. Any entrepreneur who has been there will attest to the fact that it's an overwhelming and disheartening experience. At first it may seem easier to just give up and disappear, to wallow in your misery, but you need to gather your strength and tell yourself that *the only way through it is through it.* Then, step by step, you plow forward and keep going. Finally, a sense of optimism washes over you as you near the end of such a burdensome task. At that point you will feel a sense of accomplishment, despite the emotional sadness that comes with a failed business venture.

This same theory applies to every disheartening experience you face in life. It's inevitable that not all situations will work out as planned, an many won't come out anywhere *near* where you hoped they would. You will face struggles, and there will not be a shortcut for you to get around it. The only way through, every time, is *through.* That's where Personal Positivity comes in—this Adventure is building the tools you need to make *through* happen.

An overwhelming situation can occur in different ways. Even getting through college can be a challenge, but it becomes more difficult when "college life" gets in the way. Devan, a very bright, outgoing, second-year student changed when he joined a fraternity. As we know, fraternities can do many great things for students but can also encourage some bad behavior. In this case, Devan got caught up in some stupid activities, including drunken behavior, vandalism, and defacing public property, which led to his arrest. Facing consequences from administration and possible criminal charges, he didn't know what to do. His first inclination was to drop out of college and go home to his parents where he could forget all about school and do nothing. The problem was that if he followed this plan—dropped out of school and went home —the ensuing downward spiral would likely lead to no good.

Devan might have continued this bad behavior and found a litany of excuses if his life didn't eventually turn around. He could blame his troubles on the university, claim he was falsely accused, or that because of what happened he could not get a good job or make a decent living. He would then fall back to the much-overused phrase, "It's not fair!"

Fortunately, a counselor at the school who knew about the incident sat down with Devan and helped him find a different perspective on the situation.The counselor made it clear that he would stay nearby and help Devan work through it, but Devan had to stay in the here and now. He couldn't take back what happened, what was done was done, and he had to recognize that "the only way through it was through it." The counselor told him that every time it seemed too much, Devan had to repeat that line to himself and find a way to take the next step forward.

Together, they worked through the legal and disciplinary issues with local authorities and the university. The counselor treated Devan as an adult who had to face real-life consequences for what he had done, but also ensured he knew there was a support system behind him when things got rough. In the courtroom, Devan was nervous, but he knew he would remember this moment and, with the help of the counselor, would take those lessons with him into the future and create a better life. Sometimes directly facing the consequences of making poor decisions is a way of taking positive action.

Devan graduated from the university and now has a great job. He has truly accepted Personal Positivity as his Superpower. Recently Devan called and told us he was in a company training where you had to select a motto for your life, Devan's choice "the only way through it is through it."

STAY BUSY

Life is not only about doing what you have to do, it is also about doing what you want to do to drive you forward toward reaching your goals. You'll also find a desire to do things just for fun—after all, all work and no play ...

Balancing what you have to do with what you want to do is often a function of creating balance in your schedule while staying busy. Filling your free time with positive activities makes it very difficult to get hung up on negative thoughts. Life wasn't meant for sitting around, you certainly aren't meant to be a spectator in your own life. It's time to get involved—and stay involved.

According to research from the journal *Psychological Science*, people are happier when they are busy. Activity stimulates the brain and the senses. Of course, this doesn't mean you should attempt to schedule every minute of every day, leaving no time for rest. Recharging your battery is an important part of life, but downtime cannot be the only thing filling your days. Match the positive activities and steps forward to your goals. You can take courses, do research, join organizations, go to the gym, find additional ways to learn more about your goal, and any number of other things that get you closer to that goal. If you are driven to open a small business, you can join the local business council or chamber of commerce, read books and visit websites on entrepreneurship, or find a mentor to teach you more about your industry. If you want to make a greater impact within your community, you can research different volunteering opportunities and get involved in the ones that best fit your core motivation. If you keep busy by indulging in your personal passion, you'll be surprised how much your level of energy and enthusiasm will increase.

Dennis, a high school math teacher, looked forward to having the summer free to relax and do whatever he wanted. Just like his students, he couldn't wait for two months with no daily schedule keeping him boxed in. Typically, Dennis loved the first few weeks of summer break laying in the sun and sipping cold beverages. But by about the fourth week, boredom set in. His family was busy—the kids were at camp and his partner was working as a curator at a local museum. Another week or two and he couldn't wait to get back into the classroom. For his first few years in teaching he would make the best of it, finding things to do around the house and in the neighborhood.

By the third summer, Dennis grew tired of the unfulfilling activities that filled his hours. Instead, he wanted to work toward one of his larger goals—travelling more. He wanted his children to experience faraway places that neither he nor they had ever seen. With the motivation to travel with his family, Dennis applied for a six-week summer job as a camp director. This would provide the extra money necessary to take his family away for ten days at the end of the summer break on some wonderful trips.

Dennis' story is a reminder that simply "being busy" is not enough. Your "busy-ness" has to serve a couple of objectives. One is to keep the mind active and away from getting caught up in negative thinking. This explains why many teachers take on other activities during the summer months and why retirees try to stay busy. Many researchers agree that stimulating the brain (as well as the body) is important, which won't happen if you remain inactive. For example, the 2016 research study called "Frontiers in Aging Neuroscience" reported that people who stay busier as they age are stimulating their brains and have better scores on tests of memory and cognition.

The second objective of keeping busy is to move yourself forward on the Adventure to accomplishing your goals. Dennis first recognized the benefit of being busy, and then realized that the best way to be busy was to do something that mattered, something he was passionate about and motivated to do.

Like many people, Dennis put up signs and pictures as reminders to motivate himself to keep working toward his goal. If you are visual by nature and prefer visual motivators, this might be a good tactic for you, as well. Dennis put up photos of places where he could take his family on vacation. Other folks prefer sayings, slogans, or quotes. Whatever keeps you moving forward rather than sitting around is fine as long as it motivates you to stay on your Adventure. You will be amazed how quickly any thoughts of sitting around doing nothing will disappear.

Oh, and in case you were wondering what Dennis has been up to—in the years after he made the decision to get busy achieving his goal of travelling more, his family visited Iceland, Ireland, Montreal, and toured the Pacific Northwest from the mighty redwoods of California up to the top of the Space Needle in Seattle.

Of course, your path to a busy, Positive life won't be without it's challenges. You'll meet people who want you to binge television shows with them all day or spend hours playing pool or hanging out at the local bar day in and day out. You might call these people "blockers" because they are blocking you from moving forward. We all experience blockers who get in our way. They doubt your commitment, don't have a positive attitude, and don't understand the path you are on. Do not let such people stop you from staying busy and following your path. Don't allow them to block you from working toward your goals. Remember, you decide everything for you, including whether or not you let yourself get blocked.

When you're living with Personal Positivity, it can't just be an idea. It must translate to actions that move you forward. Small actions, medium actions, big actions, actions that build, and actions that you just have to *get through* in order to get where you want to be. Approach it all with energy and enthusiasm, ditch procrastination, and make it happen.

EXERCISES FOR GUIDEBOOK 4

1 Challenge yourself: are you approaching life with energy and enthusiasm? How are you reacting to new tasks and assignments or meeting someone new?

2 Write down one example of how being energetic and enthusiastic worked for you.

3 Make a quick list of things you have been putting off; now next to each task write down a plan and time to get them done so you do not procrastinate

4 "The only way through it is through it." Write it down, post it on your wall, send yourself a reminder, and when faced with a challenge keep on going!

5 Add one activity to your week, read an hour a day, take a daily walk, go to a weekly church meeting, go out for dinner on Wednesdays.

6 *WIN TODAY!!* At the end of each day challenge yourself. Ask yourself: Did I win today? Did I get the most out of today? Did I move forward/make progress today? Did I use the precious resource of time wisely? Did I give away any smiles? Did I receive any smiles?

SAY IT!

IN THE LAST GUIDEBOOK we talked about how important it is to exhibit the power of Personal Positivity through your actions. We emphasized the importance of doing everything with energy and enthusiasm, even the things that are not particularly enjoyable. We noted the need to avoid procrastination, which can slow down forward progress at work or in anything you do. In addition, we pointed out that when you are up against overwhelming odds, you must do whatever it takes to get past such obstacles by keeping in mind that the only way through it is through it. And finally, we talked about the importance of staying busy, which is important to your mind and body and keeps you away from falling into bad habits and focusing on negativity from the past.

Now it's time to "say it."

COMMUNICATING

Throughout this Guidebook, we're going to cover various communication issues you may run into along your path as well as ones that you've likely run into along the road that led you to this point. First things first, we want to discuss the importance of speaking up and saying what is important to you, including your journey into Personal Positivity and the continued assertion of your core motivator.

Consider the saying "the words you speak become the house you live in," by the 14th-century poet Hafiz. This saying perfectly demonstrates the power words have in your life. If you have only negative things to say, you will find yourself living a negative life. Your words will reflect your outlook on life and that will be the foundation of your house. The same is true, then, for filling your world with positive words.

Often, we notice that when we say things out loud, they sound more real, more credible, and more powerful. When people seek out help from therapists, counselors, or spiritual leaders, it is often to speak about feelings and issues they have largely kept inside.

Speaking, however, is not just about what you say; it is also about how you say it. Therefore, it is important that you remain aware of how you present yourself. You want to speak clearly, make eye contact with the person (or people) to whom you are speaking, and exude confidence. You should also be careful not to ramble, preach, or come across as condescending.

We recalled a colleague at work telling us that after meetings people kept coming up to him and asking him, "Why are you so upset?" or "What is wrong?" He was shocked. Everything was perfectly fine! It was simply the way he said things: the tone of his voice, the use of words or inflections, and he had no idea he was conveying this negative message.

In addition, it is important to be appropriate in what you say, where you say it, and how it sounds. You want to speak loud enough so your intended audience, which may be just one person, can hear you, but not so loud that an entire restaurant hears you. It's also important to know when it is the right time to broach a topic and when it is not. For example, you might avoid discussing a controversial topic at a social gathering with people that you know don't share your views. This isn't to say that you should never have difficult conversations, or that you should never communicate a contrary opinion in a situation where you know it won't be received as well as you would like—it's simply about using your discernment to understand when a difficult conversation is doable and when it would be detrimental. If it is likely to be the latter, it's probably best to avoid that topic for the time being.

In addition, it is also imperative that you know when to talk and when to listen. Other people can present interesting ideas and open some great conversation topics, if you let them. Don't make every conversation all about you: listen and learn from others. Let other people tell you about themselves. In almost every social situation, if you wish to be part of the conversation, there's an expectation that you contribute as well as allow space for others to contribute, too. If this is a struggle for you, try heading into every party or dinner with a couple of stories already in mind that the particular audience at the gathering might appreciate.

That being said, speaking up is not always the best choice in every situation. If your primary motivation for speaking is to let out a burst of emotion, you may find it more beneficial to keep your silence for a few moments. This will allow the intensity of emotion to pass and allow you to formulate a response that addresses the root of the problem. A colleague of ours came into the office with a smoothie and told us that the woman behind the counter making it was an older lady who was having a hard time using the smoothie maker. It took forever and he wanted to yell at her, but he stopped himself and realized that it's just a smoothie, the woman was just there trying to make a living, and that he would forget all about it five minutes later. If he had acted on his emotions and yelled at her, or made a nasty comment, it might have stayed with her all day. If you are truly upset about something that you feel *is* important, select a time to discuss it after you have calmed down, put your emotions on hold, so you can have a rational and thoughtful conversation. Yelling in anger doesn't really help in most situations.

"SAY IT" IN A POSITIVE MANNER

Beyond the concept of "say it" is saying it in a positive manner. How you verbalize your thoughts, ideas, and opinions can have a huge impact on how your message comes across. Many people approach communication with a negative attitude and are disappointed when they don't get the desired results. Consider the likelihood of a wedding following a proposal that goes, "You wouldn't want to marry me, would you?"

Business coaches, consultants, and positive thinkers have become mindful of avoiding certain phrases such as "I can't," "It won't work," "It's so difficult," "We'll never...," "That will take forever," and so on. This is not speaking with Positivity. Sometimes it's just a matter of changing a word. Instead of "I can't," try "I will," instead of "Yes, but..." try "Yes, and...," or instead of "I'll try," say "I will." A simple change like this unlocks a serious power that will serve you well on your path to Personal Positivity.

Another key to positive communication is learning to reflect the positives in other people as well. Especially if your larger goals include leading teams, this is an extremely important practice to perfect. Many bosses speak to their employees only when they've done something wrong, and do not acknowledge their positive contributions. A perfect example comes from a school superintendent in North Carolina who worked with four associates to manage several area schools. One by one the associates contacted the agency that placed them in the superintendent's office and complained that they didn't like the environment. They felt that the superintendent didn't like their work. The head of the agency called the superintendent, whom he had known for years, and asked if he had a problem with the staff. He responded that he had no problems with any of his staff and was, in fact, quite pleased with their work. Then, as the two talked at greater length, it came out that he had never expressed his positive views of the staff. He had only criticized them when they did something wrong. The superintendent was aghast at his own behavior and his failure to say anything positive to the people working for him. He sat down with his staff and apologized. He told them that he appreciated the jobs they were doing and never meant for them to feel otherwise. This simple action went a long way toward repairing the rift between him and his employees. Positivity isn't something you're meant to keep to yourself. It should extend to those around you and infiltrate all aspects of your personal and professional life.

THE POWER OF FACE-TO-FACE TIME

Whenever you're communicating something of importance, speak to people directly, meaning face-to-face or at least on a phone call rather than through an email or a text. Dr. Cheryl Bauman, in her 2015 book, *Just Say It*, encouraged her readers to recognize and understand the power of the spoken word. Bauman pointed out that due to technology, people are becoming isolated by using social media and no longer engaging in face-to-face communication. This makes it even more important to actually "say it."

Numbers from the research team at StatisticBrain.com show that there are 26 billion texts sent in America every day. Make no mistake, the texting, messaging, and story sharing that is happening is in many ways a wonderful thing. It has done wonders to connect people and get people interacting on various levels. However, you can also be sure that a lot of Positivity is lost in translation, despite cheerful emojis. Statistics show that 67 percent of senior executives and managers say their organization's productivity would increase if superiors communicated face-to-face more often.

A *Washington Post* article from April 2018 showed that face-to-face requests are 34 times more effective than those sent by email, and that a physical handshake promotes cooperation and influences negotiation outcomes for the better.

A 2011 MIT study using electronic devices indicated comparable results, showing that "35 percent of the variation in a given team's performance was explained by the number of times team members actually spoke face-to-face."

There is greater depth and a stronger connection when people speak in person. In this age of multi-globalization, communication has changed drastically. After face-to-face conversations, which are difficult in global companies, come video connections, which have a stronger impact than conference calls. While texting is the norm for "touching base" or less significant conversations, the rule of thumb still remains that communications with greater impact are best conducted in person. High-tech communication is a great tool to utilize on a daily basis, but it's important not to forget how to speak face-to-face.

SETTING YOUR BIG GOAL

The most powerful way to say something is to ourselves, to be honest deep down inside of us. It's time to tell yourself and then others where you are going, why you are doing this, why you bought into this Adventure and began this journey to obtain the Superpower of Personal Positivity! You need to set your big goal: the one thing, the big dream. You know you own it, since it can only come from you. No one else can set this goal and no one can get in the way. You are responsible for your reality and you are responsible for the changes you want, and need, to make. Psychologists typically define setting a goal as selecting a target or objective you wish to achieve. This is what you want, deep down, to achieve more than anything else. This is why you're here—and it's no time to dream small.

Knowing your core motivator, or your "why," is the first step in setting your big goal. When you know why you want to do something, it gives you the motivation to go for it. When you start focusing on your big goal, don't be afraid to think big and challenge yourself. After all, if you think small, you'll have small results. Do you want to own your own home? Run a marathon? Lose 50 pounds? Buy a boat? Become a lawyer? Become VP of your company? These are all terrific goals. But you can do better.

To successfully set goals, you need to make them specific. Instead of "I want to own a home," you might include what neighborhood and by what date, such as: "I want to own a home in Seattle by fall 2020." Being specific gives you a clearer idea of your path, one you can picture.

Consider David, who decided in fall 2017 that his big goal was to leave his IT job and start his own computer service and repair business by January 2019. His "why" was that he always wanted to have his own business working with computers, which was his passion. He had been building computers and repairing them for his friends since he was a teenager. David figured out how long it would take him to accumulate enough money to leave his job and support himself during the lean years of getting a business off the ground. He then made a plan to put aside a certain amount from each paycheck. He also knew it would take a year of marketing himself and building a following that understood his expertise. By November 2018, he was able to give two weeks' notice at his job and by the end of January 2019, he launched his business.

After you have determined what your big goal is, talk about it, post it on your wall, and make it part of your life. In Guidebook 7, we will break your big goal down into specific actions and plans. For now, just start thinking about what that Big Goal needs to be—what feels best for you.

IT SHOULD BE YOUR GOAL

Remember, the *only* one who can set your big goal is you. If someone else wants you to follow their goal, or has a goal set for you, it is unlikely that you will generate great enthusiasm to ever reach that place. This goal must be yours; you must own it completely.

In business, you are often asked to set goals within a company to guide you on your career progression. Such goal setting typically appears on worksheets that want you to identify your goal, list milestones, objectives, results, and so forth. The worksheet may follow the S.M.A.R.T. goal-setting method, which we will discuss shortly, but the point is that these goals are created for your employer. If your big goal is to climb the corporate ladder at that company, this exercise may help you focus attention on your actual goals. However, if your goal is to leave the company in three years and go into business for yourself, your corporate goal setting is an exercise in giving the boss what he or she wants to hear. Remember, your big goal must come from your core driver and your true passion. It's not necessarily the goal your boss wants to hear. As a result, such "workplace" goal-planning is often disconnected from your real destination. That's okay, do the best job you can with energy and enthusiasm until it is no longer part of your plan.

IT SHOULD BE REALISTIC

Your Big Goal needs to be Big (it's in the name after all), but it also needs to be realistic. It should push your limits—it should scare you, just a little. Maybe your goal is to make a million dollars. This can be realistic, but will usually take time, not to mention a lot of hard work in a worthwhile career or industry. Your big goal might be: I want to be worth a million dollars before I am 40 years old.

Whatever your big goal is, write it down. Then, we will work on creating a plan that you can follow, step by step, to achieve that goal. You'll have to determine not only the steps, but how you will achieve each step. It's no easy task, but once this entire roadmap is laid out, you'll have no questions about what you need to do next in order to get one step closer to that Big Goal.

Let's take a look back at that million-dollar goal for an example of how this might work. Rather than counting on a winning lottery ticket, how will you approach reaching that goal? Will you start a new business and work long hours to make it work? What kind of business could you start in which you could make that kind of money? Could you make money through shrewd investments? Perhaps you have great skills in an area, such as sports, or creating and developing new technology. One computer maven started making his own apps, shortly after apps started gaining popularity in 2007, and one year before the iPhone app store opened in 2008. His goal was to become successful by creating, designing, and developing apps. While in his 20s, he became a very successful app designer. He followed his passion and stayed with his goal despite naysayers back then who told him apps were just a fad.

You also need to consider whether a specific goal will, or will not, fit into your life. The app designer hit the ground running, started creating apps while he was single and in his early 20s. However, in many life situations, you'll need to balance business goals with your personal life.

Karen had a big goal to become a doctor. She also had personal goals of getting married and having a family. Karen knew that she could accomplish all three of those goals, but she had to approach them at the right time. Getting into medical school and working hard for her degree would be her first goal. She was hopeful that she would then meet someone in her last year of medical school or after she graduated. Having a family would follow. She had a plan.

Then, in her first year of medical school she met Melinda, and they fell in love. This was not part of the plan. Now Karen had to decide how she would prioritize her goals. She had worked too hard to give up on her goal of becoming a doctor. She also didn't want to lose the woman she fell in love with and hoped to marry. Melinda, meanwhile, was finishing up law school. She wanted to pursue his career as a lawyer. As it turned out, they respected each other's goals and delayed marriage until Karen was in her residency and Melinda had launched her career. Once they were well-established in their careers, they started a family. Karen had achieved her goals and supported her partner as she achieved her own.

While everything went smoothly for Karen and Melinda, very often sacrifices need to be made to achieve a goal. John Hanna, an Australian entrepreneur, author, speaker, and thought leader, founded the investment firm of Fairchild Wealth Management nearly 25 years ago. In a story on TheOracles.com, Hanna explained that when they were much younger, he and his wife could not afford to pay rent, so she and their son went to stay with his sister, while he moved back in with his mother. This was necessary so he could focus his attention on, and put his money into, building his business. It became a hugely successful company where his son is employed today. "It wasn't an easy pill to swallow at the time, but I knew the sacrifice would eventually be worth it ... I did what had to be done in order to keep building my dream," explained Hanna, of reaching his primary goal.

Only you can determine what sacrifices you will have to make, and how far you will go to reach your goal.

All of this takes us back to Personal Positivity. If you have doubts, are stuck in the past, are too preoccupied or unwilling to put in the time and effort, or are afraid to make sacrifices, you are letting negativity get in the way of reaching your goal. Therefore, it is important to follow the process, get rid of baggage from the past, accept new ideas, and be open. Remember, there is a progression: talk about the process and talk about your goals.

In Guidebook 7 we will help, and challenge, you to build specific steps that will form the pathway for you to reach your ultimate destination. To prepare, there are a few things you need to start thinking about.

POSITIVE PEOPLE

Surround yourself with positive people. Naysayers and negative people can derail you from your pathway and, ultimately, from achieving your goal. Remember, you don't have to cut these people out of your life, but you must cut them out of your sphere of influence.

People often forget that they do not have to accept everyone (even family members) into their sphere of influence. The sphere of influence contains the most significant people in their life. You can know someone but not let them influence you—if they are trying too hard to be influential in your life, you can always sever the connection if necessary, at least for a while.

Negative people don't just "bring you down." They can cause you to doubt yourself, lose self-confidence, and resort to negative habits. You cannot let people who say, "why bother?" instead of going after what they want, hold you back.

Instead seek out people who exude Positivity in not only what they say, but in how they act. Are they enthusiastic about what they do? Are they goal-oriented? Are they supportive of the goals and dreams of others? The more positive people you have in your life, the more likely you are to stay on the path of Personal Positivity and enjoy great success. It can be very uplifting to bring positive people into your life, whether they are new friends, colleagues, a life coach, or a mentor. Remember, you should always ask for help and advice from such people. You will be amazed how much easier your pathway is when you have people helping you move forward instead of blocking you.

"Always work with/surround yourself with people who help make you a better version of you. Kindly avoid those who don't," says longtime filmmaker Don Roff.

S.M.A.R.T. GOALS

Goal setting has been around a long time. Before smartphones, smart cars, and smart houses, there were S.M.A.R.T. Goals, which first appeared in a 1981 issue of *Management Review*. The acronym S.M.A.R.T. stands for Specific, Measurable, Attainable, Relevant, and Timely. It is used widely in business but includes many of the same considerations you need to include in any type of goal setting.

Being *specific* means that along with your core motivator, your "why," you'll add in the where, when, how long it will take, as well as other details.

Being *measurable* is important as you'll want to follow your plan and see where you are in the process of reaching your goal. While losing weight is easy to measure by stepping on a scale, you can also measure how much you have set aside for a down payment on buying a home, how many classes are left to take to get your MBA, or how far along you are in gathering the necessary seed money to launch your start-up. David, the app designer, measured his savings every couple of weeks on route to opening his own business.

Measuring your progress keeps you on track and lets you know if you need to work harder or maintain your current progress as you continue on your journey to reaching your goal.

Attainable means that your big goal is something within reach. This means that while this goal may be challenging, and stretch your abilities, it should be something you can achieve.

Relevant refers to how appropriate this goal really is. Therefore, you might want to reconsider your goal of playing for the Green Bay Packers if you're 50 years old or having a dog show champion if your dog is a mutt that loves chasing the mail carrier down the street. If, however, you have a goal that is within reach through planning, training, studying, getting licensed, and gathering the right resources, then it can be relevant.

Timely not only means relevant to the times in which we are living, but it also refers to having some kind of schedule or timeline in which to reach your goal. You need to check your schedule constantly to make sure you are moving toward that goal every day.

While they don't fit the S.M.A.R.T. acronym, there are a few traits that can also help you reach your goal. We discussed openness earlier in the book. If you are open to ideas, suggestions, and knowledge, you make it easier on yourself to reach a goal. With openness usually comes a dose of vulnerability. This means "knowing what you don't know" and seeking the answers. It may mean having some help along the way, especially if you have a very significant goal. Doing something extraordinary almost always requires having someone working with you to make it happen. Look at the biggest successes in business. Bill Gates had Paul Allen, Larry Page had Sergey Brin, Steve Jobs had Steve Wozniak, and Hewlett and Packard had each other to help them achieve their goals. At any level, most goals require some assistance. It's not a weakness to find the positive people who can help you get to where you aspire to go. In fact, it's one of the greatest strengths you can cultivate.

One final aspect to goal setting is flexibility. The harder the goal, the longer it may take to achieve, and the more detours you must navigate on your journey. You will not only need to go back and revisit your core motivator to inspire you, but you also may need to make alternative plans in an ever-changing world. Flexibility means you can adjust as you keep on reaching for your goal. Being positive, speaking positively, and having positive people around you will be great assets as you make the necessary adjustments to your plans.

Okay, it's time—time to set that Big Goal. It is the first exercise at the end of this Guidebook. Don't worry about how you will get there; we will get to that shortly. Because you know why you are doing this (your core motivator), tell yourself where you are going, and when you will get there. That's all you need to do (for now).

EXERCISES FOR GUIDEBOOK 5

1 Set your Big Goal. Make a list of a few things if necessary, then pick one thing, not three or four. As you master Pozzam and develop your Superpower more, you will be able to pursue multiple things at once but for now you only get one. Specifically, what is the most important thing you want in life? When do you want it? Write down what it is you want to accomplish and by when you logically plan to accomplish it. This is so important; it should take up most of your exercise time for this Guidebook.

2 *WIN TODAY!!* At the end of each day challenge yourself. Ask yourself: Did I win today? Did I get the most out of today? Did I move forward/make progress today? Did I use the precious resource of time wisely? Did I give away any smiles? Did I receive any smiles?

REVIEW IT!

CONGRATULATIONS, you've made it to the midway point of your Personal Positivity Guidebook Experience. Welcome to your midterm exam. Kidding! We're totally kidding; you won't find any tricky, multiple-choice questions here. This is more of a review session—an opportunity to reflect on what we've learned so far and review how far *you've* come in the last 12 weeks.

As you have taken the time to work on each step of the process, doing the exercises at the end of each Guidebook, the sum of what you have learned should be evident. Are things looking a little rosier when you get up each morning? Do you handle hiccups in your daily life with more grace? Do you find yourself getting angry less often, and at far fewer things? Congratulations, that means you're doing the work and it's, well, *working.* That's a big deal! Now that you're living a more positive life on a daily basis, you should be feeling good (or at least better) about the opportunities that lie ahead.

Remember, this is a journey, not a quick fix; there is no race to the finish line. Since this is not a one-hour seminar, or a ten-day weight loss plan, you need to continually check your progress along the way. Some days, heck even some weeks or months, will be easier than others. The important part here is sticking to it and re-committing every time something slides. Sliding is inevitable. What you do when you realize that's happened is what counts most.

CHECKING YOURSELF

Checking yourself is helpful in any journey, especially when one step depends on another. From the initial foundation introduced in the first Guidebook, this process is designed to have an ongoing progression with each Guidebook building on the previous one. For example, if you don't take control of your thinking, you won't be able to push out negative thoughts and replace them with positive ones. If you don't push out negative thinking, you won't be able to get rid of the baggage that holds you back.

That's why it's important to check in not only at the end of each guidebook, but as you work through the next, too. Look back at how each individual step is working for you and where you're feeling more resistance, naturally. What needs more attention from you before you can move on to the next step? Do any exercises need to be repeated? At this point in the Adventure, you should be looking at things differently. Summoning and operating from a place of positivity should feel more like second nature than it did 12 weeks ago. Making changes should be easier, negativity from your past shouldn't feel like heavy, weighted shackles hindering your progress anymore. If you're not feeling more ease, more lightness, and more positivity at this point, it's time to check your internal compass. See where you might have gotten off track and go back to the Guidebook that deals with the root of your falling-off point. Work through those exercises again and then return here, ready to move forward, when you feel the momentum building again.

THE STEPS

Before reviewing the key steps of the process, remind yourself what you are trying to achieve. This is like rereading the mission statement of a business. In this case, the Superpower of Pozzam, or Personal Positivity, as we discussed in the first Guidebook, is a fresh outlook, a new approach to life and a new perspective on the world. It's a long-term step-by-step process that will make it easier to jump on new opportunities and explore more of what life has to offer.

With 12 weeks under your belt, you should be starting to see your approach to life change. There's still work to do, of course—more changes to make, more fears to overcome, more risks to take, more dreams to chase down, more goals to achieve—but we've built a solid foundation at this point and you should be feeling the positive effects of that work.

STEP 1: TAKE CONTROL

Recognizing from the start of the process that you are in control of your thoughts, ideas, attitudes, decisions, and actions is vital to your success. No one else in your life—not friends, authority figures, partners, bosses, colleagues, or family—is in charge of your life. That's all you.

Ask yourself:

- ☑ Are you letting other people influence your thought process or decisions?
- ☑ Do you find yourself blaming other people?
- ☑ Do you find yourself thinking, or saying, "There's nothing I can do about it"?

If the answer to any of those was "yes" for you, it's time for another crash course in control. Of course, we don't live in a vacuum. It's important to take in the advice and experience of people you trust and love, but the final decision comes down to you. How you feel, what you think, how you act, what you say, the next steps you take—it's all up to you, and you alone.

Remember, Personal Positivity comes from within. We all have it; the choice is whether or not to use it. When you recognize that you have the power to take control over all aspects of your life and step up and say "I own this!" you are setting the wheels in motion. It begins in that first moment, with that first declaration. Owning it is that inner feeling of confidence. You know this is something you not only want to accomplish but you *will* accomplish. Statements like "I got this," and "no problem," indicate that you are ready to tackle what lies ahead.

Taking ownership of yourself and this process can still be a little scary. That's okay; it's a big commitment, but the process has great rewards.

You've already started the work, you're already moving forward. With each step you take on this Adventure, is your commitment growing? Is your confidence growing alongside it? If you answered "yes" to that, congratulations! That sense of ownership simply isn't possible if you don't truly know you're more than capable of taking this journey on.

STEP 2: MAKE A SMALL CHANGE

When you make the commitment to Personal Positivity, you start with a baby step, in the form of making a small daily change, something simple that is productive, positive, and easy to make part of your daily routine.

As part of this Adventure, you should have made a small daily change that was productive and in line with a goal of yours. Let's take a moment to check in on that, too.

- ☑ Did you make the change?
- ☑ Have you kept it going?
- ☑ Is it becoming a habit?
- ☑ Have you considered additional small changes you can make to further this practice?

If so, you have proven to yourself that you can make a change without incurring much, if any, stress. You should also remind yourself that this decision to make a change did not come from anyone else—it was your decision to make this Positive change. Remember, you already established that you are in control. You used that control to make that change happen. Day in, and day out. You did that. And that's something to be proud of.

If, for some reason, you made a change, but didn't continue doing it, start again, or select something else that you want to change and make it a daily activity. Taking a step back to move forward is perfectly fine. Adjustment is as much a part of this process as everything else.

STEP 3: WIN TODAY

One of the most important, overarching concepts in the entire program is the idea that we can Win Today, and that if we look at each day as a chance to squeeze the day for all it's worth, then we could win that day. Think of it like a contest with yourself.

At the end of every day you can check to see if you challenged yourself.
- ☑ Did you get the most out of today?
- ☑ Did you use the resource of time well?
- ☑ Did you make some progress toward a goal?
- ☑ Did you do something just for you?
- ☑ Did you move along the path by one small step?
- ☑ Did you take a giant leap?

You don't need to be able to answer "yes" to all of these, but you should be able to say "yes" to a few. We'd even take an emphatic "Hell yes!" for a particularly effective day.

STEP 4: CLEAN OUT THE NEGATIVITY

There are two approaches you can take in life: negative and positive. By now, we're sure you can guess which approach we're for, but let's look a little closer at why, again.

Positivity and negativity are opposing forces. Negative thoughts, habits, and behaviors are the ones that drag you down, distract, discourage, frustrate, infuriate, make you feel hopeless and work to keep you stuck. Moving forward when these thoughts are grabbing at you at every turn is impossible but moving forward is a must. So it stands to reason that in order to move forward, we must focus on positivity.

Ridding yourself of negative thoughts means attacking them with persistence and determination. It's easy to *say* that you shouldn't think poorly or negatively about yourself or your situation, but it's much harder to make it stick. Consistent positive self-talk and halted negative self-talk over time is the best way to rid yourself of negativity. It isn't quick work, but it's important.

Remember, it becomes much easier if you have positive thoughts at the ready to take their place. In time, when you get the hang of replacing negative thoughts with positive ones, you'll be able to flip the switch from negative to positive thoughts very quickly. Check-in time!

- ☑ As you have worked your way through the process, have you been successful at eliminating negative thoughts and replacing them with positive ones?
- ☑ If you recently lost a milestone you were fighting for, were you able to fret over it briefly and then say, "I'm going to find a new opportunity, now!"?

Be honest with yourself. If you need more positive thoughts to push the negatives out, make a list (mentally, on paper, or on your computer) of positive things to think about. Focus on what's good in your life, especially the simple things you enjoy.

STEP 5: ELIMINATE NEGATIVITY FROM THE PAST

One place from which we accumulate a lot of negative thinking is the past. We tend to get tied to things that have already happened, and not let go. It's critical to always remember there are no do-overs, and there is no rewind. What happened, happened and there is no changing the past. The more negative baggage we collect, the more we have available to hold us back. It's time to move on.

As we discussed in the second Guidebook, dwelling on the past does you no good in the present or the future. Your energy is much better used in planning, dreaming, and working toward a brighter future. However, in order to clear up some of that mental and emotional space, we must first purge some of that negativity from the past.

If old thoughts, and the attached negative patterns, keep coming back you can visualize a closet full of cartons and old suitcases full of negativity and watch yourself cleaning it out. In fact, you can approach the process using the same lines you might say when you really clean out an actual closet filled with old junk (hint: the answer to most of these is some version of "No).

- ☑ "Do I really need this anymore?"
- ☑ "Is this important to me?"
- ☑ "Why in the world am I saving this?"

STEP 6: STAY IN PRESENT TIME

Even if you feel like you're not living in the present, you are. Because you can't live in the past or in the future, you're always technically living in the present moment. It's the only one that exists. But remembering that and having the ability to add the perspective to that truth that impacts your daily life is easier said than done.

If the past keeps pulling you back it's time to stop, look around, and recognize where you are physically in this moment. If you're in your living room tell yourself "I'm in my living room, this person/situation/job/feeling/ problem from the past is not here and does not hold power over me any longer." Next, focus on something in your current life (something as simple as an errand to run or what's for dinner will do) to snap yourself back, fully, to the present moment. Staying in the present takes work, but it's so much less stressful than trying to live in the past.

In order to check in with yourself on this step, consider the following:

Have you had occasions where the past was dragging you down and you pulled yourself back into present time? Did you feel better? Less stressed? More Positive?

If you've had this experience, then you've already started to understand the importance of staying present!

STEP 7: FORGIVE

Another big thing we discussed over the last 12 weeks was forgiveness. The ability to forgive is a vital part of your Personal Positivity journey, but that doesn't mean it's easy. It's hard to let go of something that happened in the past that was physically or emotionally damaging. Being able to honestly forgive the other person is a major challenge, but if you can remove the blame and the anger you feel from the experience and recognize who you are today, you can start on the path to forgiveness. If you're not sure how that path is going for you, think about this:

Have you been able to honestly forgive someone? If so, you are cleaning out some significant baggage. If not, it's okay. Forgiveness is something you can continue to work on. Remember, forgiveness is not really about the other person; you don't even have to tell them that you forgive them, it's something you do within, for yourself.

Forgiveness may be the hardest part of this entire process, which is another sign of its importance. If you can continue working toward forgiveness time and time again, you'll find yourself with much more room for new, positive opportunities and experiences. Every time you forgive, you allow yourself to clear out the negative emotions and mental space that person or situation took up in your mind and heart. Consider how much space you could be freeing up when the idea of forgiveness feels overwhelming.

STEP 8: TAKE CONTROL OF YOUR EMOTIONS

In Guidebook 2, we also discussed emotions, a topic that will return throughout the book. We have many positive emotions, but it's the negative ones that can cause trouble if we allow them to take control.

When it comes to negative emotions, you need to:

1. Accept them. You have a right to feel bad, but you cannot allow these emotions to continue endlessly, or they will become part of your negative baggage.

2. Take control of these emotions before they control you. One way to do that is by learning to recognize your emotional triggers and working to change them.

Since you've already made a small change in an early step of this process, you can once again make a small change here. Do your best to eliminate triggers that make you angry. Setting your alarm clock 15 minutes earlier so you won't be stressed and angry about being late for work is a perfect (and simple) example of a small change with big results. This is a way of eliminating a trigger and taking greater control over your emotional state on a daily basis.

STEP 9: ACCEPT IT, AND BE OPEN TO NEW THINGS

In Guidebook 3 we defined acceptance as being ready to receive, to take something in, to agree to a suggestion, and believe something is right, true, or real.

Openness then refers to our personal level of acceptance across a range of situations and scenarios. When you move away from negativity and dwelling on the past, you will have far more opportunities to explore other facets of who you are and what you are capable of achieving. Ask yourself:

- ☑ Am I open to making changes?
- ☑ Am I displaying my creative side?
- ☑ Am I being more adventurous?
- ☑ Am I taking some risks?

After you have reached this step, you will see that with acceptance and openness comes being more open-minded. This will help you through the rest of the process. Being open allows you to listen to other people's ideas, suggestions, and opinions. When you are open to other views of the world outside your own, you unlock the door to a vast world of information, possibility, experience, and knowledge that wasn't available to you before.

While Personal Positivity encompasses openness and acceptance, it may be difficult to break with the status quo. Nobody expects you to be open to everything that comes your way. However, if you really want to reach your goals and grow, you need to start accepting new ideas that may be outside of your comfort zone.

After you have accepted new ideas, you will need to act on them. You can't just sit by and expect things to automatically change for you. Acceptance is a process and requires effort. This means *actively* making changes that will help you reach your goals. It also factors into an upcoming step, "Act It."

STEP 10: STOP MAKING ASSUMPTIONS AND PROJECTING

Assumptions are a defense mechanism, to a certain extent. By projecting a worst-case scenario onto a possibility in front of you, your brain thinks it's protecting you from that worst-case scenario playing out. Unfortunately, in its attempt to protect us, our brain sets us up for failure by encouraging us to miss out on so many things that might be wonderful opportunities based solely on assumptions that have no evidence to support them.

The key to getting your fear-based projections under control is to first acknowledge that they exist and be able to identify them by your thought patterns when you approach a possibility, opportunity, or choice. Once you can identify when you're projecting based on fear, you can shift your perspective and choose a different route.

STEP 11: IDENTIFY YOUR CORE MOTIVATOR

Without a core motivator you are a driverless car, moving along without reason. The core motivator is your "why" and it is at the root of your goals and aspirations. It is the cornerstone of your entire foundation for this Adventure.

You've had various goals all along, and you've probably had a core motivator driving you. But at this point you need to identify it, since your core motivator will be your driving force throughout the Adventure. What is your core motivator, or passion, that keeps you driving toward your goals? Did you write it down? If not, grab a piece of paper and do that now. Write it over and over and over again. On notebooks, on sticky notes, in lipstick on your mirror, whatever and however and wherever it creates impact.

One of the most significant reasons for acknowledging your core motivator is that it becomes your point of focus when challenges, setbacks, and obstacles arise—and they will.

At this point in the Adventure, you've probably already experienced obstacles and had to reach back to your core motivator in order to keep moving forward. We promise that it won't be the last challenge you face, but we also promise that recalibrating based on your core motivator will give you the strength to keep going.

We also noted in Guidebook 3, that as you grow and your life changes, your core motivator may change. For example, when you are young your motivator might be to become more independent. When you are older, it might be to start a business or to support your family. That's why it's important to check in with your core over time. If it feels like your motivator is shifting, that's totally fine! Just make sure to write it down again and again, no matter what it settles on for the time being.

STEP 12: ACT IT AND SAY IT!

At this point, you've worked on the mental side of Personal Positivity, moving from negative to positive thinking and eliminating the negative baggage of the past. It's time to convey positivity through your actions. Your positive attitude will now become more apparent as you infuse energy and enthusiasm into everything you do.

After you successfully move through the steps, it becomes easier to act on what you learned. It is now part of who you are as a person. You now see the world through the lens of positivity and find it easier to act in a positive manner.

In Guidebook 4, we talked about how acting with Positivity can even make unpleasant tasks more enjoyable. It's all in your attitude. If you are working your way through the process, positivity should now be apparent in all of your actions.

Living and acting with positivity also means that when you meet new people, or find yourself in a social situation, you will exude that same positive attitude.

Review your social interactions when you reach this point in the process. Do people respond well to you? Are they interested in knowing more about you? If they are, then your positivity is apparent in how you act. If they are not responding well to you, ask yourself what is standing in the way of making a more positive impression.

When you "Act it" you are illustrating to yourself and others that you are living with Personal Positivity. This will open you up to many more opportunities and possibilities.

Along with acting it, you want to Say it. Spoken or written words have a great influence on who you are and how you present yourself. Words can be powerful and inspiring, and when you say something out loud it lends more credibility. Speaking about positivity reinforces it within you and in your social circles as well.

Now that you've started the process, you can check yourself by thinking about what you have to say.

- ☑ Are you presenting your thoughts and ideas in a positive way?
- ☑ Do other people see the positivity within you?
- ☑ If you are sharing your Adventure with others, are they enthusiastic?

Positivity attracts positivity and negativity attracts negativity. What you say, and how you say it, can make a major difference in how your message is received. Be aware of how you present yourself; use positive language, speak clearly, look at the person you are speaking to, and most of all exude confidence and enthusiasm when you speak to others. Also remember to listen to the other person as well and ask questions about them.

STEP 13: SET YOUR BIG GOAL

The biggest step of the process is setting your most significant goal: this is the single most important goal you want to achieve at this stage in your life. It may be starting a business or reaching a high level in your chosen career. It may be buying a home or something else that you want to purchase. It may be about becoming less dependent on others or having the freedom to travel the world. There are many possible goals, and yours must be something you personally desire deep down in the center of your soul.

When you reach this point of setting your big goal, you will be able to see more clearly how everything in this process ties together. After you made the commitment to bring Personal Positivity into your life, and owned it, each step of the process began shaping you to make the necessary changes to reach that big goal. Setting the foundation by pushing out negative thoughts and cleaning out the negativity from your past freed up your mental energy to proceed smoothly along the path to Personal Positivity. As you replaced negatives with positives, and began making small changes, you recognized how such small changes can help you reach bigger goals.

Through acceptance and openness to change, you broadened your horizons by adding new tools to your arsenal, such as curiosity, creativity, and being open to new ideas. These attributes made it easier to set your sights on achieving the bigger goal you have set for yourself. "Acting it" put your positivity into action with energy and enthusiasm while "Saying it" vocalized and legitimized your commitment to the Guidebook and provided more determination to reach your big goal. Knowing your core motivation provided you with "Why," and that will push you to maintain your commitment to your goal. Everything works together in the process.

As we also discussed, there are parameters that come with having a big, significant goal in your life. A big goal also must be challenging, stretching, realistic and time specific.

WHERE ARE YOU IN THE PROCESS?

At this point of the Adventure you should be able to look at the progress you have made thus far. Look at the steps you have conquered and the ones ahead of you. As you pass each step, your belief and commitment will continue to grow.

Of course, you will be tested along the way. Not by us, but by the world at large. The more you are committed to following this path, the easier it will be to deal with the naysayers and negativity you will encounter from others. Remember, just as you control your thoughts, they control theirs, so if they choose to be negative, that's on them.

Hopefully, since starting this process, you are now becoming aware of positive and negative people in your life. Positive people will help pull you up and provide you with motivation, intentionally or unintentionally. Negative people leave you feeling unmotivated, apathetic, and doubting yourself.

Unlike a real midterm, only you can grade how well you are doing at any point in this process. If you are mastering each step, keep on moving forward. If you need to go back and work harder on one or more steps, or you need more time to determine your big goal, take the time you need.

It's all part of the process, and taking each step of this Adventure with careful consideration and honest self-assessment is key to unlocking the true potential of your Pozzam and creating a sustainable life filled with positivity.

EXERCISES FOR GUIDEBOOK 6

1 Go back to any steps you may have skipped or had trouble with along the way. It's not unusual to get so excited about the progress that you bypass a step. The problem is that missing a step can come back later to get in your way. Review the list of steps in this Adventure and literally take a pencil and check off the steps that you feel good about having passed, and circle those you have not accomplished. After you have gone back and worked your way through the missed steps, erase the circle and put a check mark.

2 Write down three changes that this process has already helped you make in your life. They may be small changes, but they are occurring because you are living a more Positive life than when you started this book.

3 *WIN TODAY!!* Are you challenging yourself at the end of each day? Did I Win Today? Did I think about and do something for me today? Did I move forward/make progress today? Did I use the precious resource of time wisely?

ADVENTURE GUIDEBOOK #7
CONNECT IT!

IN GUIDEBOOK #5, we introduced the need to set your Big Goal. This is the most significant Goal you are determined to reach in your Positivity Adventure. It should be attainable, timely, and realistic. Your Big Goal will be the focus that leads you through much of the following Guidebooks.

If you can see your Goal clearly, you're ready to make a plan that will connect all the pieces of the road to your Goal. Think about illustrated plans you've seen before—floor plans, blueprints, database models, prototypes, outlines. When well-executed, they guide people clearly and smoothly through the completion of a goal.

When it comes to your own Big Goal, you usually won't need an illustrated floor plan, but instead a detailed list. You can make such a list by first breaking your Goal into the sum of its parts, or Goal Chunking. "Goal Chunking" is the process of breaking down the largest goal into smaller, more manageable chunks or steps that must be achieved along the way in order to reach your Big Goal.

STARTING YOUR LIST

If, for example, your Goal is to buy a home in Seattle by March within two years, your plan will include necessary steps. Make a list of each step, then rewrite your list (or move items around on your computer) so that you have a prioritized list based on the order in which you need to get things done. For example, let's suppose you decided on starting your house-buying Goal on June 1 of the current year; you'll want to create a prioritized list such as this:

- ☑ Determine how much you can afford based on your annual income and assets. (Hint: financial planners usually say a house should cost two or two and a half times your annual family income.) Do this by 6/7.
- ☑ Make a plan to start saving money for a down payment for nine months. Make the first deposit by 6/10 (or your closest pay date)—then start saving money from each subsequent paycheck.
- ☑ Visit a lender to determine how much of a loan you can get from the bank by 6/16.
- ☑ Get pre-approved for a mortgage by 7/15.
- ☑ Determine the type of house you are looking for, based on your needs (e.g., four bedrooms/three baths, a two-bedroom condo) by 7/31.
- ☑ Search for neighborhoods you like, and can afford, by 8/31.
- ☑ Look for, and find, a reputable realtor that sells in that neighborhood by 9/15.
- ☑ Look at houses that meet your needs and fall within your price range. Start by 9/30.
- ☑ Make a bid on a house (or houses if you don't land the first one) before 12/30.
- ☑ Agree upon a price with the seller 1/10.

☑ Have an inspection done by 1/20.

☑ Secure your mortgage with your lender and purchase the house before 3/1.

This is your first step. making a high-level plan, then listing it in order of what you need to do next. If you run into trouble, ask someone who has purchased a home what they did first, second, and so forth. Ask them how long the process took. Most Big Goals have been attained by someone you know, or you can look online for the process of buying a home, a car, getting into a good college, starting a business, and so on.

Recognize that some aspects of your plan will depend on other people's availability. For that reason, be realistic in setting dates. You want to move along steadily to your Goal, but you also want to do things correctly. Keep trying to reschedule meetings and appointments as soon as possible so you can stick to your plan. When working on a Goal that already has a deadline, like applying to colleges and starting college in late August, you'll want to work backwards from the dates set forth by the schools. Therefore, you need to look at the date applications are due and determine how long it will take you to complete the application and send it.

ACTION STEPS

Next, you'll want to break everything down once more into the action steps, or specific tasks, that you will need to undertake.

REMEMBER TO MAKE ALL ACTIONS TIME BOUND

For example, if you look at #4 on the list above, "get pre-approved for a mortgage," you can then list the action steps, starting on 6/16:

1. Find your tax returns and W-2 statements from the past two years on 6/16.

2. Gather recent pay stubs that show steady income by 6/18.

3. Look for documents that show additional income by 6/21.

4. Find your recent bank statements and any investment account statements that indicate you have money for the down payment. Do this by 6/23.

5. Get your credit scores from the three major credit bureaus (TransUnion, Equifax, and Experian) by 6/26.

6. Provide a means of contacting someone from your place of employment so that a lender may reach out to them to verify that you are still employed (this could be your manager, someone in HR, etc.). Do this by 6/29.

7. Research different types of loans (The SBA, FHA, VA, and other loans are available). Do this by 7/2.

8. Look up lenders and/or get referrals from someone you know and trust. Do this by 7/4.

9. Make calls/send emails and talk with lenders by 7/10.

10. Choose a lender and meet to get pre-approved by 7/15.

While this is a more complicated example of breaking down one area on your list into action steps, the idea is always the same—think through each step of the process, and what work must go toward that step to ensure it is completed fully and correctly.

This is exactly how the process works, no matter how Big the Goal or how long the journey; everything can be broken down again and again into simple, doable tasks that move you further down the path to accomplishing your Big Goal. The process takes dedication, a time commitment, and an ongoing effort. A positive attitude goes a very long way toward helping you on this journey. It makes it easier to find something that you can accomplish each and every day that leads toward your Goal. No excuses, just action. By doing this, you can Win Today and every day.

Don't allow yourself to get frustrated with the small tasks you will need to complete. These little tasks are the starting points to great accomplishments. Often these first tasks are not very exciting. Starting a business might begin by standing online to get a business permit. Building a house may start with buying and inspecting a plot of land. Staging a musical might start off by visiting a bunch of worn-down old theaters and audition studios. These are not necessarily the most exciting tasks, but they are all important starting points. As noted earlier, take a positive approach, and try making all tasks enjoyable.

DO YOUR ACTIONS DEMONSTRATE YOUR PRIORITIES?

If you are sincere about working toward your Goal, anyone who knows you should know what your priorities are based upon your actions. We find it interesting when we hear someone say, "My priority is to maximize my income at work by taking on increased responsibilities." Then the person frequently shows up late for meetings, does not ask for extra projects, rarely does anything to get more exposure with the right people in the company. Clearly, their actions do not indicate that moving up the ladder and maximizing their income at that company is really a priority.

You must ask yourself if you are taking the appropriate actions on a daily basis to reach your Big Goal. For example, if you are ready to speak with mortgage lenders on your quest to buying a home, but you have not even looked for names of lenders online or gotten any referrals in the past two weeks, how can you say this is a priority? You are not working toward your Goal.

Most people are busy with jobs, school, and/or family obligations, but doing what it takes to go through the steps on your list is imperative and you must find the time for your action steps. It can take as little as 15 or 20 minutes a day to make the necessary calls and texts or send out emails. It may mean running out of the office on your lunch hour to meet venture capitalists who might invest in your business or having lunch at your desk and registering for classes to go back to school. If you are serious about your Big Goal, you must make the extra effort.

Consider Susan who, at the age of 30, decided to go back to college to complete her degree in accounting. Financial needs had caused her to quit school after just one year and she always wanted to return but was never able to do so.

Now, Susan had made it her Goal to finally get her college degree and she was going to make it happen. She knew it would take time since she would need to attend classes after work and on weekends. So, in the spring of 2014, she set her Goal to save up money and return to school in the fall of 2015 to get her long-awaited college degree by the spring of 2018. Her Goal was achievable, and her time frame was realistic.

The first thing Susan did was make a list of the steps to achieving her Big Goal. Her list included:

1. Start setting money aside for school from her weekly paychecks the eight months prior to August 2015 registration.

2. Select a school that offered an accounting degree. While setting money aside she gave herself two weeks to do her daily research.

3. Review various schools and make a selection. For this she gave herself three more weeks to learn what she could and visit classes.

4. Select accounting courses and enroll—this was predicated on when the fall classes were listed. Once the class schedule was

made available, she gave herself three days so she would not be shut out of any classes she wanted to take.

5. Attend classes, and study regularly.

6. Continue steps 4 and 5 each semester.

7. Complete courses and graduate by June of 2018.

Breaking her list down into smaller tasks for each step on Susan's master list might look something like this:

 # 3: REVIEW VARIOUS SCHOOLS TO MAKE A SELECTION
(SHE GAVE HERSELF THREE WEEKS FOR THIS STEP, OR 21 DAYS)

1. Decide whether to attend school in person or online—review pros and cons of each. She gave herself three days to research and decide.

2. Research schools for those with classes in my area of interest. Susan gave herself three days to do this.

3. Network with others on social media who have attended the schools. For this she allocated two more days.

4. Create a list of the top three possible schools—this was done in two days.

5. Look at the websites of these schools for:
   ☑ Enrollment requirements and eligibility.
   ☑ Specific classes offered and times.
   ☑ Distance to and from school/neighborhood (if looking to attend classes). For this she gave herself two days.

6. Visit top three schools of interest (she was looking to attend classes). To make arrangements and visit three schools she set four days aside.

7. Make a selection and enroll. Susan allotted herself three days to review materials and decide and two more days to enroll.

Susan set her Big Goal, chunked it down, and then made a list of action steps that she could accomplish by daily activities. And she completed her tasks in the 21 days she had allotted for this step.

It's also very important that when you take action steps, you take notes. You want to be able to refer back to the realtors you spoke with, or the colleges you considered attending. You want to get names and contact numbers from websites and from whomever you speak to.

Remember, these small actions, or tasks, are very important. They require time and effort. If you keep your core motivator in mind (why are you doing this?), and approach each task with energy and enthusiasm, you will always be making progress. Also keep in mind that the only way to guarantee that you won't move forward is by doing nothing.

NARROWING DOWN THE FIELD AND FLEXIBILITY

Often, pursuing your Big Goal will mean learning what you don't want, or need. Don't get discouraged—remember, you only want to buy one new house, find one realtor, one school to attend, one car to buy, one career path, and one place to work (for now).

Many people get frustrated when they proceed through action steps and don't get immediate results, such as locating a house or finding a great job. If you take an action step and it doesn't work out perfectly, don't wait around for results. Instead, jump right back in the game and take that step again! You may look at dozens of houses, ten colleges, or go on numerous job interviews before achieving your goal. Narrowing down the choices through your action steps is how you get to where you want to be. Maintain your energy and enthusiasm because you are making progress by narrowing down the field of possibilities.

In order to make it to your Big Goal, it's important to maintain flexibility. No matter how much preparation you've done, chances are things will not go exactly to plan. As you go through your action steps, you may have to readjust, especially when things happen that are out of your control. For example, you might find your ideal house only to be outbid by another buyer. This is a disappointment, but there are other great homes. Now you want to focus on everything you have learned about buying a house. You simply need to readjust and go back to the step of looking at houses and start again.

If your goal is to start your own business, you may need to be flexible if you find that your industry of choice is oversaturated or, conversely, has lost its relevance. If you love to travel and your goal has been to start a travel agency, you are entering a field that has been largely replaced by technology. Many travelers now book every phase of their trips online. Does this mean your dream is dead? Of course not. It means you may have to rethink your plan from having a storefront business to serving as a travel planner or travel designer. These travel professionals work from an office (possibly a home office) and orchestrate trips, often for more affluent clients who still want the human touch. Instead of making money on commissions, which has long been the standard for travel agents, you will make money charging customers a fee for specific travel services that may include anything from reservations at fine dining establishments to private tours of ancient ruins. It's all about flexibility as you work on your plan.

You may also find that steps may overlap. You might walk into your realtor's office to discuss the specifics of the house you are looking for and find out that he or she can save you time researching the neighborhood, the cable providers, and the best schools. This way you can check off three action steps all at once and then give yourself a Big win for the day.

TO SUMMARIZE

When you decide on your Big, attainable, realistic Goal, complete with a reasonable time frame, you must develop a strategy for accomplishing and attaining it. You then chunk it down into the things you need to accomplish, and then break it down and prioritize your list. Next you break down your list further into actionable steps (or tasks) that need to be completed. You get busy working toward you goal, step by step, task by task on a daily basis.

It's almost like doing a jigsaw puzzle. Typically, you start with a plan to separate the outside pieces and make the frame, then you separate the different colors and start putting the pieces together. Sometimes they connect and sometimes you need to try again. As they connect, you see more and more of the puzzle coming together. In the same manner, you will see your goal coming into focus as you complete each step and sub-step of your action plan.

CONNECTING WITH YOUR WORLD

Connecting is not only about connecting the pieces as you work on your Big Goal, it is also about connecting with the world around you. First, you need to embrace your own Superpower. This means feeling good about who you are and your positive outlook on life. It also means feeling a sense of pride that you have adopted a positive lifestyle.

Guidebook #5 covered "saying it," so this is your opportunity to start talking to more people, especially other positive-minded people who share your outlook on life. Connecting with others starts by making an effort to be sociable, which translates to joining clubs, organizations, associations, groups, the local chamber of commerce, and so forth. Look for places where you are likely to find people with similar interest to yours—that will enhance the opportunity to strike up conversations. You might even opt to coach a team, get involved in a nonprofit, or in local politics, local charities, or in your children's school. Then start up the conversations. You have nothing to lose and plenty to gain by making the effort to meet more people.

Many people today are building up their personal and business connections through social media sites like Facebook, Instagram, Twitter, and LinkedIn, among others. While this is certainly a great way to connect with people and build up your network, it should be just one manner of meeting people and not your only source of social connections. Although a Zoom or similar call is at times a necessity and a wonderful alternative, meeting people in person is a stronger connection—eye contact, gestures, emotions and a smiling face are not always as easy to capture over video. And no, emojis don't quite have the same effect as a real smiling face.

Saying hello to people you meet in the course of your day, such as fellow dog walkers or other runners, is a positive step toward being more social. Talk to people at the gym, or at least say hello. The more often you connect briefly with people, the more likely it is that at some point, you will stop and converse.

Then, just as businesses need to maintain steady customers, you need to maintain your connections, whether they are friends or acquaintances. Remain enthusiastic when you see them, listen attentively, make the other person feel important, and let your Positivity shine (but don't overwhelm people). Remember the old saying "If you want a friend, be a friend."

If you start taking people for granted or start looking at your phone more than the person you are with, you jeopardize your connection.

Connecting with people is so important—embrace your environment, strike up conversations. By connecting with more people, you are opening new doors and opportunities through new relationships.

EXERCISES FOR GUIDEBOOK 7

1 Make a list of the major steps you will need to take to reach your Goal—then go back and organize it into what steps you need to do first, second, third, and so forth.

2 Take your larger list and start listing specific actions that you can do on a day-to-day basis. List as many actions as you will need to complete the task. Don't forget the little things, such as taking notes when making phone calls.

3 Say "Hi," to a few people you don't already know but encounter in the course of your day.

4 Join a club, organization, association, or group that interests you, and look for more ways to get involved beyond simply joining.

5 *WIN TODAY!* At the end of each day challenge yourself. Ask yourself: Did I win today? Did I get the most out of today? Did I move forward/make progress today? Did I use the precious resource of time wisely? Did I give away any smiles? Did I receive any smiles?

LOOK IT!

IN THE PREVIOUS GUIDEBOOK we talked about connections and how you need to make a plan and have a strategy to achieve your goal. To do this, you must break (or chunk) your path to your Big Goal into smaller parts. Next, you need to take those smaller chunks and break them down into action items. Then, by systematically following your plan and completing all the action steps, you will have all the connections necessary to reach your big goal.

We also talked about the importance of connecting with people around you, and engaging in face-to-face communication whenever possible. To connect with more people, it is beneficial to put intention into your appearance, not only so they can see that you take pride in yourself and to illustrate your Positivity, but because, a lot of the time, looking good also makes you feel good. That notion is what we'll be diving into for this Guidebook.

LOOKING GOOD

Kids like to play dress-up, sometimes putting on mom's or dad's clothes and sometimes dressing as someone whom they admire. Why do they do it? Because it's fun and makes them feel good.

As we get older, we dress appropriately for where we are going while still honoring our personal style. You don't wear the same clothes to a wedding reception that you wear to play softball. But looking the part is not only about dressing to fit the occasion. It's also about dressing in a way that makes you feel good. When people feel good about how they look, it gives them self-confidence, self-assurance, and Positive energy. They wear these attributes along with their clothes.

Looking and dressing well isn't about wearing expensive designer clothing. In fact, it's not even about spending money. When you dress and groom as if you don't care how you look, you risk sending the message that you aren't motivated to take care of yourself.

In an era of home offices and telecommuters, many people have a ten-second commute from their bed to their office. Many people find that taking an extra minute or two to change from pajamas to actual clothing also changes their mental approach from lying in bed to doing work.

As Judy Heminsley, founder of the *Work from Home Wisdom* blog, wrote in a July 2015 article in the British newspaper *The Guardian*, "the beauty of running a business from home is the freedom to wear whatever you want to work ... For some, wearing more formal clothes is important to get into the right mindset." For others, you may not need to go as far as to dress formally, but swapping your pajamas for something a little more structured does have an impact on mindset and motivation.

Business psychologist Helen Fisher adds that "clothes can affect how we feel about ourselves and this is also true when it comes to work." Fisher points out that in general, "if you wake up feeling grotty [shabby] and put on clothes that reflect that, it becomes a self-fulfilling prophecy. If you put on something that raises your game, it will have a subtle effect on how you feel, think and behave." This can be likened to athletes who claim that once they put their uniform on, they are more confident and ready to perform at a higher level.

Now that you have done the work to instill Personal Positivity in your thinking and life, are working toward your Big Goal, you need to be wearing Positivity, whether you're out on the town, in an office, having fun with your friends, or home alone. We're not the style police, so chose your own look, as long as you take pride in it and feel good.

The same holds true for combing or brushing your hair, putting on makeup if that's part of your style preferences, and taking care of Personal hygiene. If you look disheveled, you will likely feel disheveled, or disorganized, and not take Positive steps toward your goal.

In the end, it's all about dressing to feel good about yourself. It matters what you wear and how you look but confidence is your best accessory.

And that's what it's all about.

GETTING FIT

Physical activity and a Positive mental attitude are absolutely connected. Whether you start your own exercise routine at home or join a gym, the Positive results will be evident in your body and mind. Over the past several years, there have been a wealth of studies, reports, and articles linking physical exercise to mental energy, attitude, good moods, and even Positivity. A 2019 article on HealthGuide.org sums it up well: "People who exercise regularly tend to do so because it gives them an enormous sense of well-being. They feel more energetic throughout the day, sleep better at night, have sharper memories, and feel more relaxed and Positive about themselves and their lives."

The goal is to find some physical activity you enjoy, and are currently capable of doing, and start getting into the habit of doing it several times a week for a set amount of time—enough to get the benefits, but not so much that you are hurting yourself. Some people like walking outside and some like walking on a treadmill. Others like to bike, hike, lift weights, shoot baskets, go rowing, or alternate between several activities. Of course, you should start out slowly and build your routine as you go.

Working out does not have to be a chore, not in the modern era of mobile entertainment and health clubs with all sorts of amenities. For years many people have been working out to music or listening to audiobooks. At home you can catch up on a favorite TV show you missed.

You may also find that working out with others keeps you motivated.

Besides building muscles and losing weight, exercise can *literally* make your face look better, which may contribute to a better self-image. On her blog, Kerry Benjamin from StackedSkincare.com, writes that after working out, "you may be sweaty and tired, but your skin is glowing! Exercise doesn't just improve your overall health; it can greatly benefit your skin as well." Benjamin goes on to explain that "sweat purges your body of toxins that can clog pores and lead to blemishes. Exercise allows your sweat glands to increase their functions and get rid of those toxins. But don't forget to wash after sweating!" She also explains that "the more muscle tone you have, the healthier your skin will look and feel. Your skin has better support from strong, firm muscles, and increased muscle tone will lead to firmer appearing skin."

Along with exercise, you should try to make good food choices when it comes to your diet. While Positivity includes enjoying some of your favorite foods that simply taste great and make you happy, moderation is always the key. There are also some foods that are recommended for boosting Positive thinking. Florida-based dietitian and nutritionist Carol Aguirre suggests changing your diet by adding some foods for Positivity. Not unlike making the small changes mentioned earlier in the Adventure, making a few new food choices, and sticking with them, can also lead to other good (and Positive) habits.

When it comes to bread for your sandwiches, Aguirre points out that whole wheat has been associated with lower rates of depression. "The thing to remember, is that if you're looking for an emotional boost from your bread, it's important to stick to whole grain varieties," says Aguirre, adding that mushrooms, kombucha, eggs, and chocolate are also recommended for your list of foods to boost Positive thinking. Herbal teas, fish, greens, beans, and fruits are also among the Positivity boosters often recommended.

The key to a successful diet is finding an approach that makes you feel good and that you feel good about. You need not be a fanatic, but you can definitely enhance Positive energy through your diet.

TAKE PRIDE IN YOUR SURROUNDINGS

If you were to break into your house, take one look around, and start straightening it up, you know it's time to clean.

Yes, your surroundings should matter to you. A clean environment is part of a Positive attitude. This doesn't mean your home has to be spotless, but when you hire a cleaning person and they need a flamethrower to get through the mess, you might consider setting aside some time to straighten up.

When it comes to having a clean, neat living space, you'll find a wide range of variations. Some people, even those who are successful, don't mind living in a disaster area. In some cases, they will go crazy straightening up (which often means hiding the filth) when company is coming over. Then, the next day, it's back to looking like a postapocalyptic movie set.

On the opposite extreme are people who have a place for everything, and everything MUST be in its place. They are perpetually cleaning up, which is less a sign of Positivity than a compulsion to be in a spotless environment—this may be a means of overcompensating for another problem area. In some cases, you will find people living in homes that look like they are out of the pages of a decorating magazine. These high-end homes may resemble a museum setting without the velvet ropes. Often this is more about showing off than Positivity.

"The truth is," as Becky Rapinchuk points out in her book *Simply Clean*, "your home will never be 100% clean and organized and lived in at the same time."

The key is to maintain a home in which you can have a sense of pride. This has nothing to do with having people over; it's about a functional, enjoyable living space that shows that you put some of your Positive energy into it. A clean environment leads to more Positivity. How clean is up to you—it's about making the effort with energy and enthusiasm. Make your bed, keep the dishes from piling up in the sink, pick up stuff that ends up on the floor, vacuum on occasion—all basic stuff. This should extend to the front porch and the backyard if you are living in a house. Take pride in your whole living experience.

In business, you will see some offices where everything is in shambles. Desks overloaded with papers; old, unused furniture all over the place; and remnants of last year's Christmas party still around in July. This is typically not the sign of a good working environment. Often, you cannot do much about the building, if you don't own it, but your office space can be neat. It doesn't need to be immaculate, but there should be some sense of organization and cleanliness.

A company can be both functional and inspire Positivity. There's a great story about an employee heading to a job interview in Brooklyn, New York. As he walked from the train station to the address, not far from the East River that separates Brooklyn from Manhattan, he began noticing more garbage, a couple of abandoned vehicles, and buildings that were in need of repair. He couldn't help but think, this is getting depressing—why couldn't I have had an interview in Manhattan? The address was that of an old business on the corner, near the river, and as he entered, he became a little more disenchanted walking to the short staircase in front of him illuminated by a single lightbulb hanging from overhead. There, on the door was the sign of the company. He was certainly not expecting much. But when he opened the door only to find a spacious loft with sparse, but modern, furnishings and the latest technology, he was quite relieved. As it turned out, the people running the company could not yet afford Manhattan rents, so they opted for a lower rent in what was soon to be a growing neighborhood in Brooklyn. They were Positive-minded, fun to work with, and made it clear from their surroundings that they were enthusiastic about growing their company. The setting inside illustrated the enthusiasm, energy, and Positivity of the company well and clearly.

The reverse also holds true. A business manager recounted his frequent visits to offices in various parts of the country. The look of the office would give him a good idea of how much pride they took in their organization. What he found most disconcerting was that in some cases, even when they knew that he was coming, the place was still a mess when he showed up. "They can't even make an effort to clean up?" he'd wonder. If this was how they looked, even at their best, they clearly were not taking pride in what they were doing. This attitude very often reflects on the success of the business.

While a new up-and-coming business might not have money for top-of-the-line furnishings or elaborate décor, it's the effort that counts. Like the start-up in Brooklyn, you can do the best with what you have. Getting rid of old boxes, cartons, and broken furniture is simple, as is clearing off desks enough so you can actually see the desk.

But we want to be clear—this Guidebook isn't about spending money to make yourself or your space look better. It's about taking pride in yourself and in your home and office spaces.

How you look, how your home looks, and how your office looks are all ways to elevate your self-image and feel a little better, too.

Personal Positivity is all about you ... you've changed your attitude inside, now live it on the outside. Take pride in you and your environment and Look It!

EXERCISES FOR GUIDEBOOK 8

1 Look in the mirror and decide whether what you see makes you feel Positive or negative. If it's Positive, then you are dressing for Personal Positivity; if not, change your clothes, brush your hair, or do something simple that makes you feel good about yourself.

2 Walk around your house or apartment as if you were seeing it for the first time. Does it look neat and clean? You're not looking for perfection or the Good Housekeeping seal of approval, just your own seal of approval. Does it give you a Positive feeling? If not, take an hour and straighten up. Then look again.

3 Look around your office or place of business. Even if you are one of millions working in a cubicle, it can be neat and you can take pride in your work space. When you sit down and look around, does it make you feel good? If not, take a little while and make it more to your liking.

4 *WIN TODAY!* At the end of each day challenge yourself. Ask yourself: Did I win today? Did I get the most out of today? Did I move forward/make progress today? Did I use the precious resource of time wisely? Did I give away any smiles? Did I receive any smiles?

CHANGE IT!

ONE OF THE REASONS YOU STARTED THIS PROGRAM in the first place was so things could be different in your life. That means you wanted to make some changes, and thus far, you've already made some. Having moved through many of the steps toward Personal Positivity, you have gone from learning the fundamentals to living with a positive attitude. The first change you made, early in the book, was a small change which should now be a habit. You have also changed the manner in which you think, going from more negative thoughts to more positive ones. And don't forget we discussed being more accepting and open. This too was a change. Clearly, with a new positive attitude and having embraced greater acceptance, making changes should now be a little easier.

At this point, you should be focusing on making the changes that will help you reach your big goal, including breaking down your big goal into smaller chunks and then into action steps. But this is not the only way in which living positively progresses your life. You can also use positive change to put a little more spark in your life. After all, your new positive attitude deserves to get out and about! Leaning on your positive attitude will make trying new things more enjoyable. Keep in mind that a boring routine, or a life of doing nothing, is a breeding ground for negativity.

Even though you have already made some changes, the idea of making new changes can still come with a lot of mixed emotions. Change may be scary, fun, intimidating, exciting, uncomfortable, and/or exhilarating ... sometimes all at the same time. Change in general can be difficult because, as Gustavo Razzetti, author of the book *Stretch for Change,* says, "We can't anticipate the outcome." In a September 2018 article for *Psychology Today,* Razzetti reminds us that "although we reject uncertainty, we do have the skills to change and evolve." He also adds, "Your life is not a book written by others—create your own storyline. If you want a different outcome, start by changing your mentality. You are not just a character; you are the author of your life." This takes us back to what we said very early on in this adventure: you are in charge of you; nobody else can make decisions about your life. If you want to change, it is your call.

THE 60-SECOND RULE

Always live by the 60-second rule. The trick to change is first determining what changes are important to you, and then getting through the first 60 seconds. That's the toughest part. A lot of people are so scared of taking the initial step that they freeze up. Remember as a child when you learned to swim? The first time you let go of mom, dad, your instructor, or whoever was teaching you was scary. Then you started moving those arms and legs and pretty soon they couldn't get you out of the water. You've made many changes since then. Perhaps you changed schools; then, once you got older, changed jobs. Do you recall the first introduction to new people who would later become part of your life? It may have been scary meeting those people for the first time. But, after you got through the first 60 seconds, everything got much easier.

CHANGES FOR REACHING YOUR BIG GOAL

Author, editor, and businessman Steven Covey, in his book *The 7 Habits of Highly Effective People*, talked about asking yourself, "What is the one thing that, if you did on a regular basis (something you aren't doing today) would have the greatest impact on your life?" He would then say: "Ask yourself why aren't you doing it." Give it some thought. It's likely that you can think of "the one thing" to put first on your list of what you will do!

When you think about your big goal, you can look back at the list we discussed with the smaller steps that will lead to that goal. Together, such steps will be very impactful. This may involve learning new things through webinars or classes, or perhaps improving yourself physically. It might mean networking with the right people who can help you get the job you want, or reaching out to investors to get the seed money to start your new business. At this point, you should already be making changes to reach your big goal.

Changes are also easier if you tell people about your journey, your goal, and the changes you are making to get there. Talking about your plans will increase the chances that you will succeed. That's another reason why we told you in an earlier Guidebook to "Say It." Talk about the changes you have made, or are planning to make, write about them, share them with others. Positive-minded people will encourage you, and ask how you are doing with your changes, your journey, and reaching your goal.

A wonderful story that ties many of these ideas together comes from a woman named Catherine who was downsized from an office job she had enjoyed for 20 years. With few choices of employment, she took a rather mundane part-time job as a bookkeeper for a small neighborhood store. When not at work, the once very active Catherine spent most of her time on the sofa playing games on her phone while snacking. After several months of noticing such inactivity, her family and friends began to worry. Catherine had put on weight and was breathing heavily even after walking up six steps to her front door. She knew she needed to get in better shape, and certainly wanted to do so before she turned 50. Yet she remained unmotivated. Finally, a good friend convinced her to prepare for a local race, a 5K that was several months away. It was a terrific goal (running the race) while losing weight as she trained.

Catherine liked the idea and developed a plan. Once her plan was developed, she told her friends and family that she was committing to run this race in May. She explained the plan, laying out the action steps she would take to meet this goal. It didn't take long before her friends and family started asking her questions. Are you eating better? How is your training going? Did you run yesterday like you told me you were going to? Before she knew it, she had a whole team behind her, providing encouragement and support. If there were any naysayers, she simply blocked them out.

For several months, Catherine stuck to her plan, training for the race while losing weight along the way. She even asked people to sponsor her so she could raise money to give to a local children's hospital. By May, she was pumped up, slimmed down, and ready to run the race, having lost over 25 pounds because she changed her diet and changed her lifestyle from couch potato to athlete in training. She ran the race, finished it, and gave $1,200 to charity. She felt great both mentally and physically.

Catherine knew she was never going to lose weight just by saying "I'm going to lose weight." The race was a great motivator, and training for it gave her an action plan. In addition, her friends and family kept her driven. Losing weight is a terrific big goal, and one many people share, but you must chart a path and do the work. Just like attaining this superpower, it's a process, an attitude, and a lifestyle.

SLIPUPS

At some point you will slip up while making changes; it is inevitable. Perhaps you were drinking four cups of water every day, but you stopped doing so on a busy weekend. It's okay. You're forgiven. You slipped up, but guess what? You don't have to go back and start this entire journey all over again. Nobody is kicking you out of Pozzam. People do slip up; it's part of being human. What's important is not that you got off your desired track, it's that you don't stay off of it, you pick up where you left off and focus on you next action step with renewed vigor.

The problem is, if you slip up and start beating yourself up over it, or go so far as to give up completely, you are robbing yourself of the positive results of all your hard work. This is the number one reason why people fall off the path and never complete their journey to Pozzam. It's critical that you remember this path is not a straight line. If you have a setback, make a mistake, or hit a speed bump in the process, you need to take a deep breath, put it behind you, chalk it up to being human, and continue on your journey. You wouldn't stop a cross-country trip if you had a flat tire or ran out of gas, would you? It's the old "get back on the horse" theory. Bouncing back and moving forward after a slipup is where your Personal Positivity comes into play. Tell yourself, out loud if necessary, "I'm going to stay the course and finish the journey."

You also cannot let rejection stop you. So you didn't get into your first choice of college or law school. Move to your second choice; don't give up on your education. If you made an offer on a new house and it was rejected, don't just walk away; make a counteroffer. Consider the goal of J. K. Rowling, who was a struggling single mom determined to reach her big goal of being a published author. Rowling's first Harry Potter manuscript was rejected 12 times. Had she given up after any one of those bumps in the road, she would never have become the legendary writer of the Harry Potter series, which sold 450 million copies. Even worse, so many children would never have developed an interest in reading. Do not doubt yourself—one of the most significant aspects of Personal Positivity is believing in yourself.

This is where you might need some outside motivation. It can come from friends and relatives, which was the case for Catherine. Or as in the story of Denise in the first Guidebook, put up photos, posters, or other reminders of why you are doing this. Remembering your Personal motivation is a great way to get past speed bumps, slipups, setbacks, or rejections. Remind yourself of your "why."

You also need to keep self-doubt in check. Doubt is an emotion and we can control emotions and fears since they come from inside of us. In addition to squelching your own doubts, you cannot let other people's doubts slow you down. You can keep the doubters in your life if you wish, but you need to repel their negativity. It's kind of like the bullets bouncing off Superman. Your superpower, Pozzam, lets their doubt bounce off you.

If that doesn't work, you may have to bid them farewell, at least for the time being.

There was a woman who went through her mail, then tossed it on the kitchen table and picked up her phone to call her neighbor: "I heard about your party to celebrate big changes in your life, but I guess my invitation got lost in the mail."

Her neighbor replied calmly, "It didn't get lost ... you were one of the big changes."

TRYING SOMETHING DIFFERENT

Besides making changes to reach your big goal, you'll find yourself wanting to change things up a bit by trying something new. Maybe you love to cook and want to try making something you've never made before. Perhaps you want to try a new restaurant serving a cuisine you've never tasted. Maybe you want to reach out to someone you've never spoken to before, visit a museum or an art gallery, make plans to go camping or hiking or biking or something you don't typically do. Staying positive is much easier when you make life more interesting. Having new, stimulating experiences is very uplifting and positive.

Of course, what's fun for one person might not be fun for someone else. One person might enjoy the thrill of hang gliding while someone else will prefer the challenge of entering a chess tournament. The choice of what kind of changes and new experiences you want to take on is up to you, but whatever you do, be all in. Don't find excuses not to try doing something that really interests you. Not everything will become a habit. In fact, there are Personal challenges and goals you might just want to do once. People often have the goal of running a marathon but once they've achieved that goal, despite being very proud of their accomplishment, they never want to run one again, and that's okay!

When it comes to making changes that aren't directly related to your big goal, go for the ones that will make you feel good about yourself and your life. For example, cleaning up your environment (at home or at work), trying a new look, joining a club, taking dance lessons, learning a new language, or taking Tae Kwon Do classes may have nothing directly to do with your big goal, but such activities will enhance your positive attitude and that's terrific. Doing new things is an important part of Personal Positivity because you feel alive, especially if you remember to approach new activities with energy and enthusiasm.

EXERCISES FOR GUIDEBOOK 9

1 Make a list of changes that you have made while on your journey to Personal Positivity. Start with the small one we mentioned early in the book. Are you sticking with that change? If so, circle it, then circle other changes you have made along your journey. There are probably more than you anticipated.

2 Now list five changes you might make that aren't part of your big goal, but things you'd like to do to "shake things up a little."

3 Make a list of people who doubt you. These are people who spread negativity. You can keep them in your life, but remember to let their doubt bounce off you.

4 *WIN TODAY!* At the end of each day challenge yourself. Ask yourself: Did I win today? Did I get the most out of today? Did I move forward/make progress today? Did I use the precious resource of time wisely? Did I give away any smiles? Did I receive any smiles?

DECIDE IT!

IN THE PRIOR GUIDEBOOK we talked about the ability to make changes. Of course, only you can decide whether or not to make a change in your life. Since you've been on the path to Pozzam, you've made several changes, based on your own decisions. For example, you decided on the small change you would make on a daily basis. You later decided on your big goal. Now it is time for you to decide the most important things.

- ☑ You need to decide to expect a lot out of yourself.
- ☑ You need to decide to succeed.
- ☑ You need to decide to accomplish what you set out to do each day.
- ☑ You need to decide that you will get the most out of every single day.
- ☑ You need to decide that you will be the best you can be, each and every day.

Expect and demand big things out of yourself, make no more excuses, waste no more time rationalizing, and spend no more time working up to it. Expect results out of yourself now! You should be like the seasoned golfer who expects every putt to go into the hole, or the business owner that built and grew the business and now expects tremendous sales numbers. You have gone through the learning process, and put in the hard work. Now you must not settle for anything less than complete success.

After you have made the decision to demand the most out of yourself, you will face many more decisions and you must expect that you will make the right decisions. If not, you should be disappointed. You face decisions every day, easy ones like what to have for breakfast, what to wear to work, or whether or not to go to the gym. In addition, on a less frequent basis, you face more significant decisions, such as what car to buy, what graduate school to attend, whether or not to accept a new position at work, or whether it's time to start your own business. Decision-making should be easier for you now than when you started this journey. At this point, you have eliminated negativity in your thinking, and moved from dwelling on the past to living in present time. Most importantly, you know where you are going and what you must do to get there.

When it comes to making decisions, you want to be positive and say "yes" more often. However, you don't want to simply say yes to everything. That's not Positivity; it's just foolish. Keep in mind when you say yes, you might be giving a positive response to something negative, such as getting your money tied up in a pyramid scam or even something simple, such as agreeing to watch a movie on Netflix when you have important work to get done.

Remember, your best decisions are the ones that keep you on the road to achieving your big goal. This means saying no when it's the better choice. Let's suppose you are looking to open a business, and someone offers to go in as a partner. You then do your research and learn that your potential partner is a con artist. In this case, your best, and most positive answer, will be to say, "No, thank you." Likewise, if your goal is to lose 50 pounds, saying yes to things like ice cream, doughnuts, and cheesecake will provide negative results, and adding those extra pounds will make it harder to pull up your pants. Positive decision-making is about being able to draw those lines and determine which "yes"es and which "no"s will keep you on track toward your goals. It's about prudent discernment rather than just saying yes to everything that crosses your path.

MAKING SMART DECISIONS: DO YOUR HOMEWORK AND WEIGH YOUR OPTIONS

Confidence and Personal Positivity are wonderful traits, but they do not mean that you suddenly know everything. In most circumstances we need to get more information to make smart decisions. We check the weather before deciding what to wear, scan a few pages before deciding what book to read, or check various prices before making an important purchase. All of these decisions are ways in which we gather more information before making a decision. Larger decisions, such as where to go on vacation, means doing more homework. Therefore, Positivity means having the self-confidence to make smart decisions based on gathering information, weighing your options, and determining the best answer. The most successful people know what they don't know and are determined to find the answers. Positivity means expecting that you *will* find the best answer.

We've all heard people say, "seek and you shall find." This familiar saying has validity. A negative person will ask "why bother?" or say, "it's too much work." You, however, can seek out people who can help you make the right decisions. Perhaps a mentor or a professional, such as a doctor, accountant, or lawyer can provide the guidance you need to make your decision easier. Perhaps you'll learn from articles, websites, or webinars. You can ask the advice of friends or neighbors with the necessary expertise to help you make a good decision. Having learned how to maintain positive people in your life, you should now have people available to help you weigh the options when you have difficult decisions to make. Seeking advice is not a sign of negativity or weakness; it leads you to make the best decision.

Then once you make a decision, act on it. Do it, say it, buy it … do whatever it takes. Don't wait around, don't delay, and definitely do not procrastinate.

Earlier in the book we talked about the need to rid yourself of procrastination. You should now be able to take charge quickly, without putting it off. "I'll decide tomorrow, or the next day or the one after that," is the typical refrain of a procrastinator when faced with a decision. Paralysis by analysis is a more elaborate means of procrastination, in which you delay making a decision by overanalyzing, or researching, the topic. If you are looking to buy a new car, you'll lose out to another buyer if you take forever comparing cars on the internet. Being a positive, confident, and informed person, you will decide what you like and don't like about the car and the price, weigh the pros and cons, and make a decision without delay. Acquire the knowledge you need, then decide it and act!

FEAR OF SUCCESS

Often, when making decisions, people hesitate for one of two reasons. First, there is fear of failing because of making the wrong decision. That's understandable. You are seeking a successful outcome and emotionally you fear that a wrong decision will lead to a poor outcome. You must maintain control over your fear of failure and remain positive that your decisions will lead to good results. Don't give in to fear. Tell yourself that failure is not an option. Say it out loud.

What people don't anticipate is having a fear of success. Such a fear is a counterintuitive, rather subtle, concept that sneaks up on you when you strive for success but aren't sure if you are worthy of it, or can handle all that accompanies success.

Fear of success is nothing new. In fact, back in 1915, Sigmund Freud wrote an essay called "Those Wrecked by Success." He wrote about the "surprising and even bewildering tendency of some people to fall apart precisely when a deeply rooted, and long-cherished, wish has come to fulfillment ... as though they were not able to tolerate happiness."

The problem isn't really about handling happiness or success. Fear of success is usually related to a fear of change, which we discussed earlier. Success, which usually comes with many perks, may also mean changes, such as being surrounded by new people, travelling more often, having less time to spend with your family, and having greater responsibilities and important decisions to make that have a far greater impact on a business or a community. Success may also mean that your words may be read or heard by many more people through articles, websites, or speaking engagements. Many of these changes make us nervous and become reasons why we fear success and the significant decisions that accompany it.

People with fear of success typically get in their own way. Consider Carolyn, a mom whose goal was to start her own line of children's clothing. She began with several original designs made from organic cotton, and then got some help manufacturing the clothing inexpensively. After only a few months in business, she showed her clothing to local investors who helped with funding to start and run a more substantial small business. At first, she ran the business from her home, with the help of a couple of friends who worked for her in a part-time capacity. Pretty soon, however, the business started growing and she wasn't sure what to do next. While she wanted to make a positive impact in the clothing market with her organic line of products, she became fearful of how her life would change if she "made it big." She grew fearful of having new people working for her, of handling a marketing campaign, and fulfilling orders. All of this, and being in a leadership role, would be new for Carolyn. The potential of success left her unable to make the decision to step up her business to the next level. Carolyn had a business at the starting gate, ready to take off. She knew it was scalable; people were already interested in her products and wanted to see more. However, she could not get beyond her own fear of success.

What can you do to get out of your own way and move forward? You can utilize your Positivity to prepare yourself for success. First, you need to determine what success would look like to you—this taps into your big goal. Focus on that big goal and visualize *your* success clearly, with details.

Next you need to decide to make a change in your daily routine—you need to act it, by practicing success. For example, if success will mean meeting new people, get out and practice by meeting some new people. If success means more people will read, or hear, your words and respond to them, you can write some articles, blogs, and comments on social media. Then read the feedback and responses. If success means you will have a higher profile and people will be paying closer attention to you, then practice looking the part, acting the part, and speaking the part. If success means taking on more responsibilities at work, practice by taking on more responsibilities outside of work. Practice living the life your newfound success will afford you. Don't let the sudden change that accompanies success throw you off; prepare for success in advance. This way, instead of fearing it, you'll remain positive and embrace success.

A popular television sitcom had the lead character win a prestigious prize that he had been working toward his whole life. Yet, after he won it, he could not adjust to how it changed his life. He literally hid from reporters and treated his friends poorly. And sure, in this case that led to some audience laughs and a happy ending, but the point is, the show clearly illustrated how success and reaching a big goal can be more than you anticipated. Use your Personal Positivity to prepare.

Carolyn took a positive approach to getting past her fear of success. She started dressing for success, meeting new people, and talking with folks in the clothing industry. She went through the responsibilities that growing the company would entail and little by little she planned and practiced each one. She began living the success she anticipated, and in time, her fear of success began to dissipate. Maintaining the positive focus that she always had about reaching her big goal, she went on to have a highly successful online children's clothing business with national and international sales.

Just like living with Positivity, you can enjoy living with success in everything you do. Even though you're just practicing at first, the more you feel successful in your life, the less fearful you will feel when you attain the success you have been striving for. Don't sell yourself short. Be the positive, successful person you want to be.

DON'T LET EMOTIONS MAKE YOUR DECISIONS FOR YOU

At 10:30, Dennis decided to go to the local bar for drinks with his buddies. Dennis was worried about a presentation the following morning and gave in to the idea that his anxiety would subside if he had a few drinks. So rather than going to bed at his usual 11:30, he hung out at the bar with his friends until 1:00, then stumbled into the house and fell onto the bed nearly knocking his partner right off the other side. When the alarm went off at 6:30, he could barely drag himself out of bed, get dressed, and get to work. He was hardly ready to make an important presentation. Yet he somehow managed to drink a cup of black coffee and make it to the conference room at 9:00, looking a bit disheveled. Meanwhile, two of his coworkers were quietly betting on whether or not he would make it through the presentation without throwing up.

Dennis managed to make it through with no incidents, forgetting a few key points and giving a subpar presentation. He had a big goal of working his way up to Senior VP of Sales. This poor display was not going to move him any closer to achieving that big goal.

It all hinged on one decision for Dennis: Do I go out drinking and stay up late or do I stay home, get a good night's sleep, and be upbeat and positive in the morning? Dennis let his emotions, fear and anxiety, make that decision for him.

We talked earlier in the book about controlling emotions and not letting them control you. When it comes to making decisions, we often make bad ones when intense, negative emotions take over. As motivational speaker Mario Teguh says, "Never make a decision when you are upset, sad, jealous, or in love." There is the story of Robert, who was on his way to his big goal of buying a house. After looking at the perfect house several times, he was extremely excited. But he realized the listing agent had listed a dishwasher that did not exist. He got so worked up and angry that when the agent tried to apologize and explain it was the her mistake, Robert still thought he was being taken advantage of and he walked away from the deal. It was most likely a simple mistake and could have been easily resolved if his emotions had not gotten in the way. Robert did not make the best decision for accomplishing his goal because he acted on his emotions.

Sometimes even the most positive people let emotions trip them up, especially when it comes to making smart decisions. Ask yourself:

- ☑ If I make this decision, how will it affect the path I'm on?
- ☑ How will this affect the steps I'm going to take?
- ☑ How will it affect my chances of achieving my big goal?

Sometimes it will have no effect, other times it may even be positive, but often, if a decision is triggered solely by emotions, it can have a bad result, as it did for Dennis and Robert. A few weeks after the mediocre presentation, Dennis was passed over for a promotion that would have helped him climb up the ladder to senior VP. The good news for Robert was that he realized the issue was emotional, demanded more of himself, and went back and made a deal. Robert is now living in his dream house!

Ultimately, the biggest decision you made thus far was to start, and follow, this process. You decided to make a change in your life, and that's what you've done. Having learned so much, you are now fully able to expect high standards for yourself, and not accept anything less. You've worked very hard to get here. Now decide to expect nothing but success from yourself!

EXERCISES FOR GUIDEBOOK 10

1 Make a list of decisions you've made today. How many will help you reach your goal?

2 When you visualize success, does it worry you? If you seem fearful, what are five things you can do to practice living with the success your big goal will bring?

3 What was the last time the most positive, right decision you made was to say "no," or "no, thank you"? Remind yourself that while you want to say "yes" more often, you also know the positive power of saying "no."

4 *WIN TODAY!* At the end of each day challenge yourself. Ask yourself: Did I win today? Did I get the most out of today? Did I move forward/make progress today? Did I use the precious resource of time wisely? Did I give away any smiles? Did I receive any smiles?

LIVE IT!

NOW THAT YOU ARE LIVING WITH POZZAM, you should be seeing the difference in your life as you approach everything you do with a new Positive attitude. You should see the difference manifesting itself in your daily activities. In fact, you should be attacking each day, making plans, acting on those plans, and seeing Positive results. Procrastination, negativity, and excuses should be a thing of the past. Not only should you be living with Personal Positivity, but you should be enjoying what you are doing each day more than ever before, even the small tasks. One of the best parts of Pozzam is appreciating the little things you do because you now approach them with enthusiasm and energy. Truth is, a Positive attitude can rival any energy drink on the market when it comes to giving you an extra boost to keep you going, even when you feel tired.

This Guidebook is a check-in. It's an assessment of how you are doing today, an opportunity to look at your life right now and see how far you have come. Consider the following:

- ☑ Are you making plans to reach your big goal?
- ☑ Are you taking Positive actions?
- ☑ Do you find that you are more accepting?
- ☑ How are you handling adverse situations?

☑ Are you trying new things?

☑ Are you taking more pride in your appearance?

☑ Are you taking pride in your home and office?

☑ Are you living in the present as much as possible?

☑ Are you smiling more?

If you say yes to these questions you are right where you're supposed to be, living with Personal Positivity. Think about some of your recent activities; you will immediately see how the steps you have taken are manifesting themselves in your daily life. If there are things you have not been doing, you can also add them to that which has become a part of your life. If, for example, you haven't been trying too many new things, make a plan to check out a new type of cuisine for dinner tomorrow night, or make an effort to talk to someone new.

There are so many marvelous aspects of living with Personal Positivity, and there so many Positive results that people are happy to share, that we've included some here in answer to the questions we ask, such as:

☑ Are you interacting with new people?

Dina, who just finished her freshman year of college, has achieved the first part of her big goal, which was getting into a good college and graduating. She has also made more friends than she made during her four years of high school. She overcame her shyness, talked to new people, and now has a boyfriend and a couple of besties, as she calls the two friends she texts with every day. Her social interactions are making college a more fulfilling experience and inspiring her to do well in her studies.

☑ Are you fighting off distractions?

Jason, who for years fell behind at work-related projects, has seen that Personal Positivity helped him realize that falling behind in his work was because he let himself get distracted by things like negative thoughts. While still working toward his big goal, making his way through the process has helped him push past the negative distractions and accomplish much more work in a shorter amount of time.

☑ Are you keeping a distance from negative people and not letting them influence you?

Michelle who opened a sporting goods business over 20 years ago, watched the business grow very slowly, often because she followed poor advice from well-meaning friends who had their own ideas of how to run such a business. They were very negative when it came to new technology, such as the significance of a strong online presence. Over time, as Michelle proceeded on her journey, she began separating her relationship with her friends from their advice. She still went out dancing and drinking with her buddies, but she knew better than to follow their old-school, negative business advice. In time, Michelle's online busines flourished.

☑ Are you controlling your emotions?

Lorraine had never quite gotten over her jealousy of her younger brother Michael. Only two years apart, like many children they always seemed to battle for their parents' attention when they were young. But somehow, she still held on to that jealousy as they got older. Both Lorraine and Michael had corporate jobs and were both trying to work their way up the ladder. When Michael got a sales manager position, despite congratulating him, it was clear that Lorraine was jealous—she was older and thought it should be her moving up to a better position. Unfortunately, the company she worked for was not seeing the same sales numbers as the business in which Michael was working.

A couple of months later, in an effort to help his sister out, Michael called her immediately when he heard of an opening at his company that he thought she'd be perfect for. It was a higher-level position with more money than she was currently making. But Lorraine, much to his surprise, turned it down. Michael had let go of their sibling rivalry many years earlier but didn't realize his sister was still hanging on to it. Jealousy and Personal pride were controlling Lorraine's decision-making and standing in her way of moving up.

A year later, Lorraine discovered the power of Personal Positivity and reached her goal of moving to a new company with a better job at better pay. She realized that this new level of success could have happened much sooner if she had followed her brother's recommendation. She recognized that emotions such as jealousy and personal pride could have a negative impact if she didn't control them.

☑ Do your actions meet your priorities?

Have you been focusing on acting in a way that helps you reach your goal? Karen, a manager of a small tech firm in California, had a goal of changing the business culture in the company. Yet despite her Positive attitude, she had a difficult time turning her goal into a well-thought-out plan with action steps. She decided to spend a week simply observing, carefully, the ways in which her team interacted to see where they were getting stuck and what was wrong that could be improved in the current culture—watching and learning was actually a first step in the process, although she had not written it down. From her observations, she saw that some members of the team spent time gossiping, others were not being very transparent, and some were simply slacking off. When she had a clearer idea where the obstacles were to a new and more productive culture, she started taking small action steps to instill the type of culture she wanted, which included transparency, eliminating gossip, and promoted the idea of helping others get work done if you had extra time, rather than just slacking off. Each day, she took a step closer to a better office culture by meeting with team members and implemented parts of the culture she wanted to initiate. These actions allowed Karen to start improving the culture in the company and get more work accomplished.

☑ Are you focused on your core motivations?

Sometimes you need to remind yourself why you are working so hard to reach your goals. Josephine, a sales rep by day and graduate student by night, spent a weekend trying to catch up on her sleep before heading to visit her mom for dinner on Sunday night. Josephine walked up the steps to her mother's house, having not seen her mom in a few weeks, all the while sending her money to help make ends meet in her retirement years. As she reached the top step, she couldn't help asking herself, "Why am I working so hard? Why don't I just take some part-time job while I finish school?" When her mom opened the door and they hugged, Josephine's core motivator came rushing back to her as she remembered how her mom worked extra hours waiting tables to help her pay for grad school. Josephine remembered that her core motivation was to take care of her mom who had done so much to help her reach her goals.

MOVING FORWARD

At every stage of life, you will find new things you want to accomplish. They don't have to be big goals, like climbing Mount Everest or starting a multimillion-dollar tech business. Small goals are so important; they are the things that keep us going from day to day and maintain our Positivity. Martin, an 86-year-old retired widower in Florida, says that getting up and dressed each day, reading the newspaper, talking to his grandchildren, walking around the neighborhood, smiling, and saying hello to people he meets, talking to his friends, and playing an occasional game of Ping-Pong—which he's still pretty darn good at—makes life fun and fulfilling. He maintains the Positive attitude he established some 45 years ago. He never dwells on past negativity and never lets it hold him back from staying in present time.

Changing your outlook and attitude was a big step, and a risky one to take. You should feel a sense of pride and accomplishment having taken the risk. But there's always more that lies ahead. As we noted early on, Pozzam is not a one-time fix or a way to achieve a single goal. It's a new attitude that stays with you even after you are standing in that beautiful house you wanted to buy and looking out the windows at your new neighborhood, or after you have graduated law school and sought your first job as an attorney. As life moves forward, you will embark on new goals and Personal Positivity will be within you, helping you reach them.

Consider Mark, who was tentative at first about starting on the path to Personal Positivity. He made some small changes but often forgot to do them and soon lost interest, reverting to negativity. He was unhappy but couldn't figure out why. He spent too much time thinking about the lost opportunity to go into his grandfather's restaurant business, and about his longtime girlfriend who had moved on with her life, complaining that he was too needy and dependent on others ... which he was.

Then one day, while working at his dead-end office job, he saw an ad online for patio furniture and recalled building an entire patio with his dad years ago—he loved designing and building the patio and even replicating the design for a neighbor. That day Mark realized that his passion was not at a desk job, but at building things like patios or decks. He decided to make significant changes in his life. That evening he started again on the road to Personal Positivity. He remembers saying out loud, "The heck with my grandfather's restaurants, I'm going to start my own patio and deck design and building company." Then he started on his way to achieving his new big goal, owning his own business. When he got started, he also realized that he was motivated to do something he enjoyed and to have autonomy. While he didn't acknowledge it at first, autonomy was his "why" or core motivator.

Working his way through the process, Mark pushed out the negativity that had slowed him down over time, which put him in a better place. He began focusing on making changes, putting down the video games, cutting down on drinking with his buddies at the bar, and started cleaning up his apartment and cleaning up his life. Now that he had a "why" and a big goal, he started making plans and acting on them. He took more pride in how he looked and started exercising at a local gym. He worked at his plan nights and weekends while holding down his boring day job until he was able to take a big risk and cut loose. He took the risk, and made a change, quitting his job to go solo with his own business backed by a couple local investors whom he met at the gym through networking.

Mark did everything with energy and enthusiasm. He had plans for each day and he stuck to them. He loved crossing off accomplishments on his to-do list, and every evening he smiled knowing that he had won the day. It wasn't a matter of whether or not his business would succeed; he 100 percent expected that it would. There was no doubt in his mind.

After three long years, he reached his goal of paying back his investors and becoming an independent business owner. Mark saw where he was going, no place, and decided that Personal Positivity would help him make the changes to be where he wanted to be. Now he is living with his fiancée in a beautiful house, with one of the patios he designed and built sitting right out back.

Mark took the journey and reached his big goal.

So now what? Does he shut down Personal Positivity? Is it just a means to an end? *Not at all!* As mentioned above, Personal Positivity is not a short-term lifestyle nor a means to an end—it's a life changer. You don't stop having goals and making plans to reach them. Of course, not every goal is a "big goal," but that's okay. You are now able to tackle all sorts of goals. For example, Mark wanted to enter a local charity tennis tournament. While he was in good shape from spending his days constructing patios and decks, he needed to spend a few more days at the gym working on stamina and strength in his legs so he could cover the court. He also needed to brush up on his tennis, since he had rarely played since his college days, more than a decade earlier. Once again, Mark took the same approach to reaching a goal, and made his plans. He wrote them down and acted upon them, confident that he would reach his goal. When the tournament came, he participated and almost won. His goal wasn't about winning; it was about playing and helping to raise money for a good cause.

The point is, now that you are living your life with Personal Positivity it will manifest itself in whatever you do, and at any stage of your life. You should appreciate how Personal Positivity permeates all aspects of your life.

Many people reach big goals when they are young, such as getting through college, then grad school, business school, law school, or some other educational or training program to excel in their area of interest. They then have Personal goals such as getting married, starting a family, buying a home, as well as career goals. People then find that they want to reach new heights at work, start their own business, or change careers entirely. These become big goals. There are also retirement goals, and even second career goals. Along the way, so many other goals from physical endeavors, to charitable goals, to Personal challenges all come into play, all of which benefit from living with Personal Positivity. So whatever stage of life you are in, keep on working toward your big goal and know that others will follow and that you can approach them with the same confidence.

Each of the areas we've discussed should now be part of your mind-set. They all play a role, individually and together, in helping you make important changes in your life. Each new goal, large or small, will be met with your new attitude; you will make a plan, follow your plan, push away distractions, and ignore bad advice—you will start out by attacking each day and by taking actions to meet your goal(s), and you will take on each challenge, or obstacle, with an attitude of "I can handle this—piece of cake!" You will not succumb to doubt or negativity but always believe that you will succeed, and that failure is not an option.

Now you can see why Personal Positivity is such a life changer. It lets you create and maintain a Positive life, without fear of change, by making good decisions and enjoying Personal successes that go beyond just monetary goals. Aren't you glad that you elected to take the path to Pozzam? Now go out and Live It, every day!

EXERCISES FOR GUIDEBOOK 11

1 Think of five ways in which Personal Positivity has manifested itself in your life over the past week.

2 If there are areas you have missed along your journey, such as trying new things, exercising, or being more accepting, make a list of ways in which you can improve that piece of Pozzam for yourself.

3 *WIN TODAY!* At the end of each day challenge yourself. Ask yourself: Did I win today? Did I get the most out of today? Did I move forward/make progress today? Did I use the precious resource of time wisely? Did I give away any smiles? Did I receive any smiles?

REVIEW IT! (PART 2):
YOUR FINAL EXAM

DON'T WORRY, once again you need not study for this exam. In fact, you should be congratulating yourself. You've made it through the adventure to Pozzam. Your life has changed, and you are embracing a new positive attitude and lifestyle that manifests itself in all aspects of your life. Of course, your Adventure isn't really over; it continues as you proceed forward with your new superpower, taking on new challenges, meeting new people, and going after new goals.

In this Guidebook, as we did back in Guidebook 6, we are going to review the steps that you have taken to get where you are. This will allow you to see if there is anything you missed along the way or you want to go back and review.

Hopefully, you have read the many examples within these pages illustrating people utilizing Personal Positivity in their lives. Of course, the stories from your own adventure will be unique to you, but these stories were included to inspire and help you along your journey.

If you have been doing the exercises at the end of each Guidebook, they should also have contributed to your successful adventure. As you have seen throughout the book, the steps to reach Pozzam built upon one another and were interrelated. Small changes led to greater comfort when it came to larger, more challenging changes, and those changes brought you closer to reaching your big goal. You should now be confident and well versed at making changes (big and small) on a regular basis and feeling good about the opportunities that lie ahead.

THE STEPS

If you need to go back and take a quick review of the first 13 steps of the process, by all means review the Guidebook #6; we'll wait. Unlike the first Guidebooks that set the foundation and started you on your adventure to Personal Positivity, Guidebooks 7 through 11 focused on your new, positive lifestyle and enhanced your life with your new superpower—Personal Positivity. These steps are much easier to incorporate into your life because of the early changes you made, especially when it came to eliminating negativity in your thoughts and moving from the past to living in present time and your life.

So, let's look at the next series of steps you have taken in the last five Guidebooks. Think about how they are working for you.

STEP 14: START YOUR LIST

In Guidebook 7, we introduced the concept of connecting it. This referred to putting together the pieces of your big goal and making a list of the steps you will need to take to achieve that goal. We used the very specific goal of buying a house in Seattle by the end of the year as an example and set about putting down each step in the home-buying process. After you made your list, which would include getting pre-approved by a lender, finding a realtor, looking at houses, and so forth, you would then prioritize the list based on the order in which you would do the various tasks. The next part of this step was what we called "chunking," whereby you took a major step such as "find a realtor," and broke it down into smaller, actionable pieces, or chunks. For example, this would include looking up local realtors and calling five each day. It would include speaking with five lenders, and so on. These are the actionable steps, or subcategories, that allow you to complete the larger steps on the road to reaching your big goal.

We also pointed out the importance of making all the actions on your list time bound, such as calling ten realtors in the next three days. Having dates by which to complete the larger steps as well as the smaller tasks is helpful. It's the reason so many of us did our homework on Sunday nights, because we had a due date of Monday morning. A time-bound list lets you hold yourself accountable, so you will work on accomplishing each task on your list by a given day. We also reminded you to keep your core motivator in mind, which will always keep you focused on your adventure.

STEP 15: CONNECT WITH YOUR WORLD

This is where you take your new superpower out for a spin, and start talking to more people, especially other positive-minded people who share your outlook on life.

However, it's not just about being more vocal about Positivity, but also about being sociable in general and joining clubs, organizations, associations, groups, and so forth. Sure, it's wonderful to connect with people online, but nothing replaces the face-to-face interactions that are so valuable in life.

Getting involved in activities in your community can also mean spreading Positivity around. This could include joining a nonprofit, volunteering at your kid's school, even tossing your hat into a local election. Being connected to the world around you and interacting with other people is a great way to stay positive and not allow yourself to slip back into old negative habits.

STEP 16: LOOK IT

When you look good, you feel good. That's why so many people look at themselves in the mirror and smile—they like what they see. As mentioned in Guidebook 8, this isn't about spending a lot of money on designer clothes; it's about taking pride in how you look, being well groomed, and wearing neat clothes. Looking good makes you feel good, whether you're working alone from home, or in a busy office, warehouse, or retail location. It also emanates Positivity in whatever you do and shows people that you care about how you present yourself.

In Guidebook 8, we also discussed how this thinking transcends to your home and workspace. Your home does not need to be immaculate, but a sense of neatness and organization also shows a sense of Personal pride. Most people make their beds every day, knowing full well that outside of their immediate family, and perhaps a few pets, nobody is going to see their neatly made bed. It simply makes them feel better to have made the bed.

We even extended this attitude to your workspace. While some people can work efficiently through clutter, your office, cubicle, or other workspace is also a representation of yourself and your Personality. Overly messy can give off the impression you don't care what others think or it suggests that other areas of your life are in disarray. "Look it" essentially means looking the part of someone who is enjoying a positive attitude and lifestyle. It shows you care about how you, your home, and your workspace look because they represent you.

STEP 17: GET FIT

One step we talked about, back in Guidebook 8, is good for you both mentally and physically. That's engaging in physical activity. This can mean anything from a daily gym regimen to running, brisk walking, creating a home workout routine, or participating in a sport, or physical activity, you enjoy. The key is finding something that is challenging, but not to the point where you will potentially injure yourself. It's about movement, motivation, stimulation, and a healthy body and mind.

Physical activity can result in losing weight, putting on muscles, building up stamina, or simply getting into better all-around shape. It's not just about physical results; it's part of Positivity, which explains why millions of people work out at health clubs before going to work. It's uplifting, invigorating, and pumps them up to start the day.

This step also includes making good food choices and finding a diet that is right for you. Besides eating the foods that provide nutrients, there are also foods that boost positive thinking, such as herbal teas, fish, greens, beans, and fruits.

STEP 18: CHANGE IT

This should have been a familiar step since you've already made a number of changes throughout the process. At this point, you're no longer making fundamental changes but focusing on the changes that will help you reach your big goal. We acknowledged that changes can still be scary, but now you should find them much easier since your attitude has changed, and you have confidence that changes will be effective and keep you in the right path.

In Guidebook 9 we introduced the 60-second rule. This is understanding that the toughest part about making a change is getting through the first 60 seconds. After that, it gets easier to adjust. Perhaps you started talking to more people as a change in your lifestyle. After the first 60 seconds, you got into the conversation, and realized that speaking with new people was not as daunting as you thought it would be. We tend to over-anticipate changes, thinking that they will be very difficult to handle. Then, after a minute, the change proves to be less scary than anticipated. Most changes fall into this category, which makes the 60-second rule so appropriate.

Changes that affect your big goal are ultimately important, but not all changes have to be big—small changes are vital, too. Typically, they add up and help you reach your big goal. It also helps to tell other people about your changes. This makes you feel a sense of responsibility to these people. After all, you don't want to let them down by not following through on your proposed changes, do you? If you let people know that you are going to find a realtor through phone calls and emails this week, you'll want to do so, not only for yourself, but to let the five or 500 people—if you're posting on social media—know that you've done what you intended to do.

STEP 19: CHANGE THINGS UP A BIT

Not every change is about reaching your big goal—there are other aspects of life that are important. Personal Positivity is not strictly a goal-oriented process. It's all about living your life with energy and enthusiasm. It's about allowing yourself to enjoy new experiences, do things you've always wanted to do, make changes you've wanted to make, go places you've wanted to go, and so forth. It's about shaking things up and doing new things with energy and enthusiasm. This step is, perhaps, the most fun, in that you get to stop and ask yourself: what is something I really want to do today, or next week, or next month? The only thing holding you back now is not knowing what you really want to do.

As we mentioned earlier, staying positive is much easier when you make life more interesting. A boring routine, like sitting around and doing the same old things day in and day out, breeds negativity. Having new, stimulating experiences is far more exciting. Do something positive for yourself. And don't forget, you get to decide what you would like to do—not someone else pressuring you or telling you what they *think* you should do. One of the foundational aspects of Pozzam (that we reiterate through all the steps) is that you, and only you, can make decisions for yourself.

When it comes to making changes that aren't directly related to your big goal, put your efforts to the ones that will make you feel good about yourself and your life. For example, cleaning up your Personal environment (at home and/or at work), trying a new look, joining a club, joining a gym, or getting involved in charitable activities may have nothing directly to do with your big goal, but these activities make you feel content, connected, stimulated, or more knowledgeable or simply provide some fun in life.

STEP 20: DECIDE IT

In Guidebook 10 we talked about the need to decide it is time to expect a lot from yourself, decide to succeed, and decide to accomplish what you set out to do each day! After all, you are at a point where you should expect to win every day.

In this Guidebook, we also discussed the significance of making smart decisions, whether they are large or small. Having a positive outlook and attitude, you should now trust that you will make the right decision based on understanding and weighing the options. You should also know what you don't know and ask for guidance from positive people when making decisions.

We reiterated the idea of saying yes more often, but not in the wrong circumstances. Sometimes smart, and more positive, decision-making results in saying no.

Fear of success also entered the discussion because many people, despite being positive, get tripped up when this unexpected fear arises. You must remain in control over this fear as you do with other emotions and remind yourself that you have nothing to fear. In fact, one way to circumvent fear of success is to practice living with what you perceive as success. This way you will not fear success when it happens—you will have rehearsed and prepared yourself for the change success can bring, just as an actor prepares to play a role—only your success will be real.

STEP 21: LIVE IT

And finally, we reached the final step, which is more than a step. Living with Personal Positivity changes your life entirely. It is the culmination of taking the adventure throughout the pages of this book, following the steps, and reaching a completely new outlook on life.

In Guidebook 11, we asked several questions pertaining to what you learned and the changes you made throughout the process. It's always a good idea to check yourself and make sure you are not slipping back into negative habits, letting emotions control you, or getting lazy and not acting in ways that move you closer to your next goal.

We also addressed one of the most important aspects of the book: longevity. Pozzam doesn't just help you reach a single big goal—it's not a quick fix. It remains part of your life and you can utilize what you have learned to reach your next goal and the one after that. Using the story of Mark, a young man who wanted nothing more than to be autonomous and run his own business, we illustrated the point that Personal Positivity stays with you, when Mark moved on to his next goal of taking part in a tennis tournament for charity. The tools he learned with Personal Positivity helped him achieve that Personal goal as well.

Remember: Positivity has no expiration date!

SO, WHERE YOU ARE NOW?

At this point, having worked through the Pozzam Adventure, Personal Positivity should be part of who you are. It will be evident in how you approach activities, decisions, challenges, and interactions with other people.

You will, however, still be tested from time to time by doubters and negative people. But don't worry, you now have the inner strength and self-confidence to stand up to such negativity. It is not your responsibility to force other people to become believers in Personal Positivity. It's a Personal choice that some people will make, and others won't—they do not want to (or are too scared to) let themselves escape negativity. You can tell your story, and even recommend this book, but just like you, other people have the power to make their own decisions.

Also, as noted earlier, you will still experience negative emotions such as sadness, disappointment, fear, frustration, and even anger. Positivity is not an escape from reality, nor should it be. The difference is that you are now able to take control over such emotions and can effectively move beyond them or understand how to work with them in a timely manner. Likewise, you will still run up against tough decisions, challenges, and situations that are out of your control, such as a Personal relationship not working out as you had hoped or losing a job. Living with Positivity can't prevent these things from happening, but it makes a notable difference in how you react and respond. Instead of sulking for three months over losing your job, you will recognize that what has happened is already in the past the moment you were handed your walking papers. Then, after a couple days of frustration, aggravation, and cursing your former boss, you will be back out there with a new attitude, ready and determined to take on the goal of finding a better job, or even making a career change. Positivity is about taking a positive approach and moving forward.

In your day-to-day life, you should now be accepting invitations and opportunities that you might have passed up before, putting yourself out there more often, doing your daily activities (even boring chores) with an uplifting, positive attitude, and continuing to improve yourself with exercise and education. You should be taking actions, reaching goals and, of course, winning every day! Yes, you now possess a superpower, and that's *POZZAM!*

Made in the USA
Middletown, DE
04 December 2021

54173716R00089